Federal Financial Institutions Examination Council

ANNUAL REPORT 2010

Board of Governors of the Federal Reserve System, Federal Deposit Insurance Corporation, National Credit Union Administration, Office of the Comptroller of the Currency, Office of Thrift Supervision, State Liaison Committee

Federal Financial Institutions Examination Council

ANNUAL REPORT 2010

Board of Governors of the Federal Reserve System, Federal Deposit Insurance Corporation, National Credit Union Administration, Office of the Comptroller of the Currency, Office of Thrift Supervision, State Liaison Committee

MEMBERS OF THE COUNCIL

Sheila C. Bair, *Chairman*
Chairman
Federal Deposit Insurance Corporation

John E. Bowman, *Vice Chairman*
Acting Director
Office of Thrift Supervision

Debbie Matz
Chairman
National Credit Union Administration

John Walsh
Acting Comptroller of the Currency
Office of the Comptroller of the Currency

Daniel K. Tarullo
Member, Board of Governors of the
Federal Reserve System

John Munn
Director, Nebraska Department of
Banking & Finance

LETTER OF TRANSMITTAL

Federal Financial Institutions
   Examination Council
Arlington, VA 22226
March 31, 2011

The President of the Senate
The Speaker of the House of Representatives

Pursuant to the provisions of section 1006(f) of the Financial Institutions Regulatory and Interest Rate Control Act of 1978 (12 U.S.C. § 3305), I am pleased to submit the 2010 Annual Report of the Federal Financial Institutions Examination Council.

Respectfully,

Sheila C. Bair

Sheila C. Bair
Chairman

TABLE OF CONTENTS

MESSAGE FROM THE CHAIRMAN

Sheila C. Bair

While the recent financial crisis technically ended in 2010, the slow economic recovery and the failure of 157 banks last year reflect that the FFIEC continues to have a vital role in maintaining the stability of the financial industry. The FFIEC has remained on the forefront of major policy initiatives that prescribe uniform principles, standards, and report forms for the federal examination of financial institutions by its member agencies. The FFIEC also continued to foster communication, cooperation, and coordination among member agencies and the State Liaison Committee that make up the Council, and its task forces, including interagency efforts to address certain provisions of the Dodd-Frank Wall Street Reform and Consumer Protection Act of 2010 (the Dodd-Frank Act).

I am pleased to report that the FFIEC continued to meet its mission of promoting uniformity in the supervision of financial institutions in 2010. Details on the 2010 achievements are included later in this report in the Record of Council Activities and Activities of the Interagency Staff Task Forces. I would like to recognize, however, some of the more significant initiatives that the Council, its task forces, and interagency working groups facilitated during the year:

- Released guidance on reverse mortgage products. The guidance, adopted by each of the financial regulators, emphasizes the consumer protection concerns raised by reverse mortgages and the importance of financial institutions mitigating the compliance and reputa-

tion risks associated with these products.

- Released an advisory that reminded institutions of supervisory expectations for sound practices to manage interest rate risk (IRR). This advisory, adopted by each of the financial regulators, reiterates the importance of effective corporate governance, policies and procedures, risk measuring and monitoring systems, stress testing, and internal controls related to the IRR exposures of depository institutions.

- Facilitated interagency guidance on correspondent concentration risks that outlines expectations for identifying, monitoring and managing correspondent concentration risks between financial institutions. The guidance also addresses expectations for performing appropriate due diligence on all credit exposures to, and funding transactions with, other financial institutions.

- Facilitated the development and publication of final interagency guidance to provide sound practices for managing funding and liquidity risk and strengthening liquidity risk-management practices. The guidance emphasizes the importance of cash flow projections, diversified funding sources, stress testing, a cushion of liquid assets and a formal, well-developed contingency funding plan as primary tools for measuring and managing liquidity risk.

- Issued updated guidance for

examiners, financial institutions, and technology service providers on the risks associated with retail payment systems. The Retail Payment Systems Booklet provided guidance on the risks and risk-management practices applicable to financial institutions' retail payment systems activities, including checks, electronic payments related to credit cards and debit cards, and the automated clearing house.

- Facilitated the development and issuance of interagency appraisal and evaluation guidelines that reflect developments regarding appraisals and evaluations as well as changes in appraisal standards and advancements in regulated institutions' collateral valuation methods.

- Released the revised FFIEC Bank Secrecy Act/Anti-Money Laundering (BSA/AML) Examination Manual.

- Trained over 2,500 state and federal employees from various

agencies through training sponsored by the FFIEC's Examiner Education Office.

- Offered a number of well-received training sessions for examiners, including several on analyzing credit risk. Also designed and piloted a new course on distressed commercial real estate and a second pilot on structured finance.

- Announced improvements in the production and distribution of the Uniform Bank Performance Report (UBPR) by transitioning these processes to the interagency Central Data Repository (CDR). These improvements facilitated the availability of UBPR data and reports to bankers, bank supervisors, and the general public through the CDR Public Data Distribution Website.

- Published various revisions to the Reports of Condition and Income, including changes to reflect the permanent increase in the deposit insurance limit to $250,000 that was enacted

in July 2010. These revisions will become effective on March 31, 2011, upon approval from the Office of Management and Budget.

As evidenced by the foregoing initiatives, the FFIEC continues to do important work—thanks to the dedicated and talented full-time Council staff, as well as task force representatives from all the member agencies. Even though great progress was made throughout 2010, we have much more work to do in the coming year, including the implementation of the SAFE Act in 2011 and the requirements imposed on the member agencies by the Dodd-Frank Act. Despite these challenges, the FFIEC continues to provide a forum for the regulators to act—in a strong and unified voice and in a timely fashion—on supervisory policy issues that are relevant and of critical importance. I am, indeed, honored to have served as its Chairman for the last two years.

Overview of the Federal Financial Institutions Examination Council Operations

The Federal Financial Institutions Examination Council (FFIEC or Council) was established on March 10, 1979, pursuant to title X of the Financial Institutions Regulatory and Interest Rate Control Act of 1978 (FIRIRCA), Public Law 95-630. The purpose of title X, cited as the Federal Financial Institutions Examination Council Act of 1978, was to create a formal interagency body empowered to prescribe uniform principles, standards, and report forms for the federal examination of financial institutions by the Board of Governors of the Federal Reserve System, the Federal Deposit Insurance Corporation, the National Credit Union Administration, the Office of the Comptroller of the Currency, and the Office of Thrift Supervision and to make recommendations to promote uniformity in the supervision of financial institutions. To encourage the application of uniform examination principles and standards by the state and federal supervisory authorities, the Council established, in accordance with the requirement of the statute, an advisory State Liaison Committee. In accordance with the Financial Services Regulatory Relief Act of 2006, a representative state regulator was added as a voting member of the Council in October 2006. The Council will see a change in July 2011 according to the provisions of the Dodd-Frank Wall Street Reform and Consumer Protection Act of 2010 (Dodd-Frank Act) which closes the Office of Thrift Supervision and transfers most of its functions to the Office of the Comptroller of the Currency. Certain other authorities of the Office of Thrift Supervision will be transferred to the Federal Deposit Insurance Corporation and the Board of Governors of the Federal Reserve System. Correspondingly, in accordance with the Dodd-Frank Act, the Director of the newly created Consumer Financial Protection Bureau will join the membership of the Council.

The Council is responsible for developing uniform reporting systems for federally supervised financial institutions, their holding companies, and the nonfinancial institution subsidiaries of those institutions and holding companies. It conducts schools for examiners employed by the five federal member agencies represented on the Council and makes those schools available to employees of state agencies that supervise financial institutions.

The Council was given additional statutory responsibilities by section 340 of the Housing and Community Development Act of 1980, Public Law 96-399. Among these responsibilities are the implementation of a system to facilitate public access to data that depository institutions must disclose under the Home Mortgage Disclosure Act of 1975 (HMDA) and the aggregation of annual HMDA data, by census tract, for each metropolitan statistical area.

Title XI of the Financial Institutions Reform, Recovery, and Enforcement Act of 1989 established the Appraisal Subcommittee within the Council. The functions of the subcommittee are (1) monitoring the requirements, including a code of professional responsibility, established by states for the certification and licensing of individuals who are qualified to perform appraisals in connection with federally related transactions; (2) monitoring the appraisal standards established by the federal financial institution regulatory agencies and the former Resolution Trust Corporation; (3) maintaining a national registry of appraisers who are certified and licensed by a state, and are also eligible to perform appraisals in federally related transactions; and (4) monitoring the practices, procedures, activities, and organizational structure of the Appraisal Foundation, a nonprofit educational corporation established by the appraisal industry in the United States.

Title V of the Housing and Economic Recovery Act of 2008 established the responsibility for the federal banking agencies, through the FFIEC and in conjunction with the Farm Credit Administration, to develop and maintain a system for registering depository institution employees as registered loan originators with the Nationwide Mortgage Licensing System and Registry (NMLSR). The system shall, at a minimum, furnish or cause to be furnished to the NMLSR information concerning the employees' identity, including: (A) fingerprints for submission to the Federal Bureau of Investigation and any governmental agency or entity authorized to receive such information for a state and national criminal history background check; and (B) personal history and experience, including authorization for the NMLSR to obtain information related to any administrative, civil, or criminal findings by any governmental jurisdiction.

The Council has six members, and in 2010 it was comprised of a member of the Board of Governors of the Federal Reserve System appointed by the Chairman of the Board, the Chairman of the Federal Deposit Insurance Corporation, the Chairman of the Board of the National Credit Union Administration, the Comptroller of the Currency, the Director of the Office of Thrift Supervision, and the Chairman of the State Liaison Committee. To effectively administer the full spectrum of projects in all its functional areas, including but not limited to researching future enhancements for reporting, training products, and guidance the Council established six staff task forces. The task forces are each comprised of six senior officials, drawn from the five federal member agencies and a representative of the State Liaison Committee; each are tasked with one of the following subject matters:

- Consumer Compliance

- Examiner Education

- Information Sharing

- Reports

- Supervision

- Surveillance Systems

The Council also established the Legal Advisory Group, composed of the general or chief counsel of each of the member agencies, to provide support to the Council and staff in the substantive areas of concern. The task forces and the Legal Advisory Group provide research and develop analytical papers and proposals on the issues that the Council addresses. In addition, the Council established the Agency Liaison Group, composed of senior officials responsible for coordinating the efforts of their respective agencies' staff members.

Administration of the Council

The Council holds regular meetings at least twice a year. It holds other meetings whenever called by the Chairman or three or more Council members.

The Council's activities are funded in several ways. Most of the Council's funds are derived from assessments on its five federal member agencies. It receives tuition fees from non-agency attendees to cover some of the costs associated with its examiner education program. The Council also receives reimbursement for the services it provides to support preparation of the quarterly Uniform Bank Performance Report.

In 2010, the Federal Reserve Board provided budget and accounting services to the Council. The Council is supported by a small, full-time administrative staff in its operations office and in its examiner education program, which are located at the Council's examiner training facility in Arlington, Virginia. Each Council staff member is detailed from one of the five member agencies represented on the Council but is considered an employee of the Council.

RECORD OF COUNCIL ACTIVITIES

The Federal Financial Institutions Examination Council in session.

The following section is a chronological record of the official actions taken by the FFIEC during 2010 pursuant to the Federal Financial Institutions Examination Council Act of 1978, as amended, and the Home Mortgage Disclosure Act (HMDA).

February 16, 2010

Action. Approved the issuance of the Council's annual interagency awards.

Explanation. The Council has an interagency awards program that recognizes individuals of the member agencies who have provided outstanding service to the Council on interagency projects and programs during the previous year.

March 12, 2010

Action. Approved the 2009 annual report of the Council to the Congress.

Explanation. The legislation establishing the Council requires that, not later than April 1 of each year, the Council publish an annual report covering its activities during the preceding year.

March 18, 2010

Action. Approved Appraisal Subcommittee Chair, Deborah S. Merkle, Office of Thrift Supervision.

Explanation. The Council is required to approve the selection of the Appraisal Subcommittee Chair, who serves a two-year term.

March 18, 2010

Action. Approved Re-Appointment of State Liaison Committee Member, Sarah Bloom Raskin, Maryland Office of Financial Regulation Commissioner.

Explanation. The Council must approve two of the State Liaison Committee members—those who do not officially represent the Conference of State Banking Supervisors, the American Council of State Savings Supervisors, or the National Association of State Credit Union Supervisors.

March 26, 2010

Action. Approved the appointment of six task force chairs.

Explanation. The chairs for all six standing task forces are approved annually and are drawn from management and staff of the five federal member agencies and representatives of the State Liaison Committee.

April 9, 2010

Action. Approved the Central Data Repository (CDR) Steering Committee's Task Order #6.

Explanation. The Council is required to approve task orders that exceed a specific dollar amount. Task Order #6 covers funds for CDR enhancements to improve Call Report processing, public data distribution, and Uniform Bank Performance Report processing.

July 8, 2010

Action. Approved proposed revisions to the FFIEC's Freedom of Information Act (FOIA) regulation.

Explanation. The Legal Advisory Group of the Council recognized the need to update its FOIA regulation pursuant to significant amendments to the FOIA since 1988,

Chairman Bair engaged in discussions during the November 2010 Council meeting.

including the EFOIA of 1996 and the Open Government Act of 2007. The FFIEC FOIA regulation has been in effect since 1980 and was last amended in 1988. The Council approved the proposed revisions and the final updated regulation was published in the *Federal Register* in December 2010.

October 27, 2010

Action. Approved New State Liaison Committee Member, David Cotney, the Massachusetts Division of Banks Acting Commissioner.

Explanation. The Council is required to approve two of the State Liaison Committee members—those who do not officially represent the Conference of State Bank Supervisors, the American Council of State Savings Supervisors, or the National Association of State Credit Union Supervisors.

November 22, 2010

Action. Approved the 2011 Council budget.

Explanation. The Council is required to approve the annual budget that funds the Council's staff, programs, and activities.

December 30, 2010

Action. Approved Memorandum of Understanding (MOU) by and between the FFIEC, Board of Governors of the Federal Reserve System, Federal Deposit Insurance Corporation, Office of the Comptroller of the Currency, and Office of Thrift Supervision regarding the management and funding of the Central Data Repository (CDR).

Explanation. The CDR is an ongoing FFIEC project and during 2010 production of the Uniform Bank Performance Report (UBPR) was added to the CDR. In order to simplify oversight of CDR operations the governing MOU was rewritten to incorporate the UBPR. That new MOU supersedes and replaces the CDR MOU dated August 2007 and the UBPR MOU dated March 2009.

STATE LIAISON REPORT

John Munn, Chairman
Director, Nebraska
Department of Banking & Finance

David Cotney,
Commissioner, Massachusetts
Division of Banks

Harold E. Feeney
Commissioner, Texas
Credit Union Department

Douglas Foster,
Commissioner, Texas
Department of Savings and Mortgage Lending

Charles A. Vice
Commissioner, Kentucky
Department of Financial Institutions

The State Liaison Committee consists of five representatives of state regulatory agencies that supervise financial institutions. The representatives are appointed for two-year terms. A State Liaison Committee member may have his or her two-year term extended by the appointing organization for an additional, consecutive two-year term. Each year, the State Liaison Committee elects one of its members to serve as chair for twelve months. The Council elects two of the five members. The American Council of State Savings Supervisors, the Conference of State Bank Supervisors and the National Association of State Credit Union Supervisors designate the other three members.

The Financial Services Regulatory Relief Act of 2006 made the Chairman of the State Liaison Committee, currently John Munn, the Director of Banking and Finance of the Nebraska Department of Banking and Finance, a voting member of the council. With the passage of this act, the State Liaison Committee appointed state supervisors to represent the state system on FFIEC task forces and working groups. The State Liaison Committee's involvement with such groups enables state regulators to participate in substantive policy discussions on a broad range of important regulatory subjects; reflecting the spirit and intent of Congress in establishing the State Liaison Committee. The Conference of State Bank Supervisors serves as the primary liaison to the FFIEC for all administrative matters.

In response to their role on the Council, the State Liaison Committee meets in person before each Council meeting to review the agenda and discuss topics of interest which may come before the Council.

In addition, to further state-federal supervisory efforts, the State Liaison Committee continues to encourage state regulatory authorities to adopt and implement those policies, guidelines, and examination procedures adopted by the Council.

In 2010, David Cotney, Commissioner of the Massachusetts Division of Banks, became the first State Liaison Committee representative to chair an FFIEC task force when he was elected chair of the Consumer Compliance Task Force in April.

ACTIVITIES OF THE INTERAGENCY STAFF TASK FORCES

Task Force on Consumer Compliance

The Task Force on Consumer Compliance promotes policy coordination, a common supervisory approach, and uniform enforcement of consumer protection laws and regulations. The task force identifies and analyzes emerging consumer compliance issues and develops proposed policies and procedures to foster consistency among the agencies. Additionally, the task force reviews legislation, regulations, and policies at the state and federal level that may have a bearing on the compliance responsibilities of the five federal member agencies.

During 2010, the task force used two standing subcommittees to help promote its mission: the Community Reinvestment Act (CRA) Subcommittee and the Home Mortgage Disclosure

Act (HMDA)/CRA Data Collection Subcommittee. The task force also creates ad hoc working groups to handle particular projects and assignments. The task force meets monthly to address and resolve common issues in compliance supervision. While significant issues or recommendations are referred to the FFIEC for action, the FFIEC has delegated to the task force the authority to make certain decisions and recommendations.

Initiatives Addressed in 2010

CRA Subcommittee Activities

After considering comments received on proposed CRA questions and answers that were published in January 2009, the federal banking and thrift agencies adopted on March 11, 2010 one new question and answer and two

revised questions and answers. These Questions and Answers (Q&As) consolidate and supersede all previously published Interagency Q&As on the CRA and were effective immediately. The new question provides examples of how to demonstrate that community development services meet the criteria of serving low- and moderate-income areas and people. The revised Q&As enable consideration of a pro rata share of mixed-income affordable housing projects as community development projects.

At the end of May 2010, the federal banking and thrift agencies approved via notational vote the 2010 List of Distressed or Underserved Nonmetropolitan Middle-Income Geographies where revitalization or stabilization activities will receive CRA consideration as community development. The agencies issued the list on June 1, 2010.

HMDA/CRA Data Collection Subcommittee Activities

The HMDA and CRA Data Collection System re-architecture initiative was completed on schedule and on budget. Benefits associated with the HMDA/CRA 2010 re-architecture initiative relative to the current mainframe system include reduced data reporting and processing costs and enhanced agency access to updated HMDA and CRA data. The project was completed on June 30, 2010.

The task force voted to approve the 2011 budget for HMDA and CRA on September 9, 2010 and

Task Force on Consumer Compliance meeting.

presented to the Council for approval.

On November 10, 2010, the task force approved by notational vote to gather and publish American Community Survey (ACS) data from the U.S. Census Bureau for HMDA and CRA purposes every five years. More frequent updates will affect the geographic income levels used for CRA examinations, which to-date have only been updated every ten years.

Fair Credit Reporting Act (FCRA)

On February 18, 2010, the task force approved examination procedures corresponding to the regulation implementing Sections 623(a)(8) and 623(e) of the FCRA regarding the duties of furnishers of information to a consumer reporting agency. The rule commonly known as the "furnisher rule" promotes the accuracy and integrity of information furnished to credit bureaus and other consumer reporting agencies. The effective date of the furnisher rule was July 1, 2010.

On November 9, 2010, the task force approved examination procedures corresponding to the regulation implementing Section 615(h) of the FCRA involving the duties of institutions that use consumer report information for risk-based pricing purposes in extensions of credit. The rule requires creditors to provide consumers with a "risk-based pricing" notice. The effective date of the risk-based pricing rule was January 1, 2011.

Regulation Z (Truth in Lending)

On February 18, 2010, the task force approved amended Regulation Z examination procedures to incorporate revisions made to Regulation Z by the Credit Card Act (effective date February 22,

2010) and the Higher Education Opportunity Act (effective date February 14, 2009).

On June 10, 2010, the task force approved amended Regulation Z examination procedures to incorporate revisions for open-end transactions (effective date July 1, 2010).

Regulation E (Electronic Fund Transfers)

On June 10, 2010, the task force approved examination procedures to incorporate changes to Regulation E covering gift cards and overdraft fees for ATM and one-time debit card transactions. The revised procedures also refer to each agency's existing overdraft guidance and include the Board of Governors of the Federal Reserve System's (Federal Reserve Board) recent clarifications to Regulation E (effective date July 1, 2010).

Regulation DD (Truth in Savings)

On July 2, 2010, the task force approved via notational vote examination procedures which were amended to reflect technical clarifications provided by the Federal Reserve Board.

Reverse Mortgages

On August 18, 2010, the FFIEC agencies published final reverse mortgage guidance in the *Federal Register* entitled Reverse Mortgage Products: Guidance for Managing Compliance and Reputation Risks. The final guidance discusses the general features of, certain legal provisions applicable to, and consumer protection concerns raised by reverse mortgage products. In addition, the guidance focuses on the need to provide adequate information to consumers about reverse mortgage products; to provide qualified independent

counseling to consumers considering these products; and to avoid potential conflicts of interest. The guidance also addresses related policies, procedures, and internal controls and third-party risk management.

Flood Insurance

In 2009, the FFIEC agencies, along with the Farm Credit Administration, proposed and solicited public comments on additional questions and answers regarding insurable value and force placement issues. During 2010, the task force completed its review of the comments. Final action on certain proposed questions and answers is expected in early 2011 while additional comment may be sought on some proposed questions and answers.

Task Force on Examiner Education

The Task Force on Examiner Education is responsible for overseeing the FFIEC's examiner education program on behalf of the Council. The task force promotes interagency education through timely, cost-efficient, state-of-the-art training programs for agency examiners and staff. The task force develops programs on its own initiative and in response to requests from the Council or other Council task forces. Each fall, task force staff prepares a training calendar based on demand from the five federal member agencies and state financial institution regulators. Based on this demand, task force staff schedules, delivers, and evaluates training programs throughout the year. In 2010, the number of people that attended task force-sponsored training totaled 2,562 (see the table on page 10 for details of participation by program and agency).

Task Force on Examiner Education meeting.

Federal Deposit Insurance Corporation's Seidman Center in Arlington, Virginia. This facility offers convenient access to two auditoriums and numerous classrooms.

Course Catalogue and Schedule

The course catalogue and schedule are available online at www.ffiec.gov/exam/education.htm.

Additionally, a printed copy of the 2011 course catalogue and schedule are available from the EEO. To obtain a copy, contact:

Karen K. Smith, Manager
FFIEC Examiner Education Office
3501 Fairfax Drive
Room B-3030
Arlington, VA 22226-3550

Phone: (703) 516-5588

Task Force on Information Sharing

The Task Force on Information Sharing promotes the sharing of electronic information among

Initiatives Addressed in 2010

The Task Force on Examiner Education has continued to ensure that the FFIEC's educational programs meet the needs of agency personnel, are cost–effective, and are widely available. The task force meets monthly with the Examiner Education Office (EEO) staff to discuss emerging topics, to review feedback from each course and conference, and to develop a framework for future conferences and courses. The solid partnership between the task force principals and the EEO staff promotes open and regular communication that continues to result in high quality, well-received training.

Specific accomplishments during 2010 for the EEO were two well received pilots of the Structured Finance and Distressed Commercial Real Estate courses. These courses have been added to the 2011 training calendar with a combined total of 15 sessions. Additionally, updates to the BSA/AML Examination Manual and the Information Technology Examination Handbook continue to be available to examiners and the industry through the FFIEC Website.

Facilities

FFIEC rents office space, classrooms, and lodging facilities at the

Calvin Moye instructs students at the FFIEC's Real Estate Appraisal Review School II.

FFIEC agencies in support of the supervision, regulation, and deposit insurance responsibilities of financial institution regulators. The task force provides a forum for FFIEC member agencies to discuss and address issues affecting the quality, consistency, efficiency, and security of interagency information sharing. Significant matters are referred, with recommendations, to the Council for action, and the task force has delegated authority from the Council to take certain actions.

To the extent possible, the agencies build on each other's information databases to minimize duplication of effort and promote consistency. The agencies participate in a program to share, in accordance with agency policy, electronic versions of their reports of examination, inspection reports, and other communications with financial institutions. The agencies also provide each other with access to their organizations' structure, financial, and supervisory information on their regulated entities. The task

2010 FFIEC Training by Agency and Sponsored—Actual, as of December 31, 2010

Event Name	FRB	FRB State Sponsored	FDIC	FDIC State Sponsored	NCUA	OCC	OTS	FCA	FHFB	Other	Total
Advanced BSA/AML Conference	1	11	61	13	7	22	16	0	0	5	136
Advanced Cash Flow Concepts & Analysis: Beyond	20	13	35	0	2	28	9	5	0	0	112
Advanced Commercial Credit Analysis	17	9	71	24	6	21	8	0	2	0	158
Anti-Money Laundering Workshop	4	19	39	17	9	0	21	0	0	8	117
Advanced Fraud Investigation Techniques for Examiners	0	6	17	3	8	6	1	1	1	0	43
Asset Management Forum	0	14	62	19	1	21	7	0	0	0	124
Capital Markets Conference	16	21	68	8	7	21	19	1	2	0	163
Capital Markets Specialists Conference	13	7	80	4	9	14	17	19	9	0	172
Cash Flow Construction and Analysis	21	11	26	11	11	28	8	2	0	0	118
Commercial Real Estate	34	8	146	25	35	48	37	0	3	1	337
Community Financial Institutions Lending Forum	9	9	39	9	3	12	6	7	0	0	94
Distressed Commercial Real Estate Analysis Pilot I	1	0	2	0	2	4	2	0	0	3	14
Financial Crimes Seminar	9	20	72	13	13	0	27	2	0	11	167
Fraud Identification On-line Training	1	0	5	0	4	6	4	1	0	1	22
Information Technology Symposium	3	0	3	0	3	4	4	0	0	1	18
Fundamentals of Fraud	0	0	6	10	3	11	7	1	0	5	43
Information Technology Conference	11	11	36	18	7	32	38	14	3	0	170
Instructor Training School	7	3	2	0	1	7	0	6	0	4	30
International Banking School	3	4	5	4	0	3	0	0	0	1	20
International Banking (Self-Study)	10	0	3	0	0	11	2	0	0	6	32
Payment Systems Risk Conference	11	6	20	5	3	20	7	0	1	11	84
Real Estate Appraisal Review School II	20	13	47	0	4	0	2	4	0	0	90
Real Estate Appraisal Review I (On-line)	2	0	8	0	2	0	0	0	0	0	12
Supervisory Updates & Emerging Issues	44	15	66	20	9	42	27	10	7	0	240
Structured Finance Pilot II	4	0	3	0	2	3	4	0	0	4	20
Testifying School	0	0	17	0	0	9	0	0	0	0	26
Grand Total	261	200	939	203	151	373	273	73	28	61	2,562
Percentage	10.19	7.81	36.65	7.92	5.89	14.56	10.66	2.85	1.09	2.38	100
Combined Agency and Sponsored Percentage	17.99	NA	44.57	NA	5.89	14.56	10.66	2.85	1.09	2.38	100

force and its working groups use a collaborative website to share information among the FFIEC agencies. The task force maintains a "Data Exchange Summary" listing the data files exchanged among FFIEC agencies and a repository of communications and documents critical to information sharing.

The task force has established three working groups to address technology-development issues, to perform interagency reconciliation of financial institution structure data, and to develop interagency identity management. In addition, the task force receives demonstrations and reports on agency, financial industry, and other FFIEC initiatives pertaining to technology development; including the production and development status of the interagency Central Data Repository.

Initiatives Addressed in 2010

Technology Issues

The mission of the task force is to identify and implement technologies to make the sharing of interagency data more efficient and to accommodate changes in agency databases and technologies. The task force's Technology Working Group (TWG) meets monthly to develop technological solutions to enhance data sharing and to coordinate the automated transfer of data files between the FFIEC agencies. The group is heavily involved with weekly tracking of the interagency exchanges given the recent transition to using XML, delta files, and Connect: Direct.

The TWG continues to develop necessary links and processes to exchange electronic documents, develop an inventory of future technology projects, and upload information to the collaborative website where documents and crit-

Task Force on Information Sharing's Technology Working Group meeting.

ical materials pertaining to interagency information exchanges are stored. TWG efforts addressed in 2010 include:

- *SNC Modernization*—All agencies completely implemented new Shared National Credit schemas and are processing XML files.

- *NIC 2.0*—Agencies began preparing to accommodate the NIC 2.0 data feed in preparation for NIC 2.0 becoming the system of record by the end of March 2011.

- *Interagency Data Exchange (IADE) Project Plan Update*— Agencies fully completed the effort to migrate data series from mainframe BulkData transfer to Connect:Direct/XML processes. BulkData is now retired.

Structure Data Reconciliation

The task force's Structure Data Reconciliation Working Group (SDRWG) continued to reconcile structure data about financial institutions regulated by FFIEC agen-

cies to ensure that the information the agencies report is consistent and accurate. The SDRWG's quarterly reconcilements have greatly resolved structure data discrepancies among the agencies.

Identity Management

In 2010, the Identity Management Working Group prepared a white paper illustrating the benefits of piloting an Identity Management technology framework within the FFIEC agencies. A presentation was made late in the year to the agencies' Chief Information Officers at one of their periodic meetings in order to gain their support for moving forward. The purpose of the document was to brief them on the new information challenges presented by the recent financial reforms, and to achieve a consensus on the scope and urgency of the efforts needed to meet these challenges going forward.

Task Force on Reports

The law establishing the Council and defining its functions requires the Council to develop uniform reporting systems for federally supervised financial institutions and their holding companies and subsidiaries. To meet this objective, the Council established the Task Force on Reports. The task force helps to develop interagency uniformity in the reporting of periodic information that is needed for effective supervision and other public policy purposes. As a consequence, the task force is concerned with issues such as the development and interpretation of reporting instructions; including responding to inquiries about the instructions from reporting institutions and the public, the application of accounting standards to specific transactions, the development and application of processing standards, the monitoring of data quality, and the assessment of reporting burden. In addition, the task force works with other organizations, including the Securities and Exchange Commission, the Financial Accounting Standards Board (FASB), and the American Institute of Certified Public Accountants. The task force is also responsible for any special projects related to these subjects that the Council may assign.

To help the task force carry out its responsibilities, working groups are organized as needed to handle specialized or technical accounting, reporting, instructional, and processing matters. In this regard, the task force has established a Central Data Repository (CDR) Steering Committee to make business decisions needed to ensure the success of the CDR initiative, monitor the project status, and report on its progress. The CDR is a secure shared database for collecting, managing, validating, and distributing data reported in the quarterly Consolidated

Task Force on Reports meeting.

Reports of Condition and Income (Call Report) filed by insured commercial banks and state-chartered savings banks. The CDR also processes and distributes the Uniform Bank Performance Report (UBPR) under the oversight of the Task Force on Surveillance Systems.

Initiatives Addressed in 2010

Reporting Requirements for the Consolidated Reports of Condition and Income

After receiving approval under the Paperwork Reduction Act (PRA) from the U.S. Office of Management and Budget (OMB) in March 2010, the Federal Deposit Insurance Corporation (FDIC), the Board of Governors of the Federal Reserve System (Federal Reserve Board or FRB), and the Office of the Comptroller of the Currency (OCC) (collectively, the banking agencies) implemented several revisions to the Call Report

in 2010. The revisions responded to such developments as a temporary increase in the deposit insurance limit, changes in accounting standards, and credit availability concerns. The reporting changes that took effect March 31, 2010, included new data on loans to non-depository institutions and on other-than-temporary impairment of debt securities, additional data on certain time deposits and unused commitments, and a change from annual to quarterly reporting for small business and small farm lending data and for the number of certain deposit accounts. Annual collection of new data pertaining to reverse mortgages began December 31, 2010. The Office of Thrift Supervision (OTS) implemented several of the same reporting changes in the Thrift Financial Report (TFR) filed by savings associations.

During the second and third quarters of 2010, the task force evaluated recommendations from the banking agencies and a bankers' association for potential Call Report revisions to be implemented in March 2011. After considering the purposes for which the banking agencies would use the recommended new or revised data and the reasons for certain proposed instructional clarifications and modifications, the task force approved the inclusion of several of the recommendations in a proposal to be issued for comment. The proposed revisions were intended to assist the banking agencies in gaining a better understanding of banks' credit and liquidity risk exposures; primarily through enhanced data on lending and securitization activities and sources of deposits. In September 2010, the banking agencies published an initial PRA *Federal Register* notice requesting comment for 60 days on the proposed March 2011 reporting and instructional changes. The OTS incorporated some of the proposed Call Report changes into a separate set of proposed revisions to the TFR for which an initial PRA *Federal Register* notice was published in October 2010.

After considering the 23 comments received on the March 2011 Call Report proposal, the banking agencies agreed to proceed with most, but not all, of the reporting changes that had been proposed. Modifications were made to some of the proposed changes in response to comments. In addition, the agencies received comments that discussed the permanent increase in the deposit insurance limit to $250,000 that was enacted in July 2010 and its implications for the calculation of core deposits in the UBPR. The banking agencies concluded that these comments would support revisions to two existing Call Report deposit items in March 2011, which would

enable the agencies to modify the UBPR's definitions related to core deposits and non-core liabilities. Following task force approval, the banking agencies jointly published a final PRA *Federal Register* notice for the March 2011 Call Report revisions in January 2011. OMB must approve these revisions before they become final.

In June 2009, the FASB established the Accounting Standards Codification as the single source of authoritative nongovernmental U.S. generally accepted accounting principles. The FASB Codification reorganized all existing U.S. accounting and reporting standards from a standards-based model to a topically-based model. During the second quarter of 2010, the task force began incorporating FASB Codification references into the Call Report instruction book. In the instruction book update for September 30, 2010, the FFIEC issued a revised glossary section of the book that adds Codification references throughout while retaining references to the pre-Codification standards. The task force expects to incorporate Codification references into the rest of the Call Report instruction book in 2011.

The Dodd-Frank Wall Street Reform and Consumer Protection Act (the Dodd-Frank Act) abolishes the OTS and transfers its functions to the OCC, the FDIC, and the FRB effective July 21, 2011, or the designated date published in the *Federal Register* by the Department of Treasury Secretary. After careful review, the banking agencies and the OTS (collectively, the agencies) concluded that having common financial reports and reporting processes among all FDIC-insured banks and savings institutions would be more efficient than maintaining the OTS's separate reports for savings

associations. Common reporting would lead to more uniform comparisons of financial condition, performance, and trends among institutions. For these reasons, the OTS decided to propose the elimination of the TFR, and the agencies agreed to propose requiring savings associations to begin filing the Call Report effective March 31, 2012. Following task force approval of an initial PRA *Federal Register* notice for the proposed migration of savings associations from the TFR to the Call Report, the agencies jointly published this notice for comment in February 2011. At the same time, the FRB published a notice of its intent to require savings and loan holding companies to submit to the FRB all regulatory reports currently required to be filed by bank holding companies beginning in the first quarter of 2012. In addition, the OTS and the FDIC jointly published an initial PRA *Federal Register* notice proposing the elimination of the OTS's annual Branch Office Survey and the submission by savings associations of the FDIC's similar annual Summary of Deposits Survey effective June 30, 2011. Finally, the OTS published a notice of its intent to cease collection of monthly median cost of funds data from savings associations effective January 31, 2012. Savings associations and their holding companies would continue their current reporting processes through the effective dates specified above.

In November 2009, the task force initiated a project to combine the two Call Report forms into one form. A single form would reduce redundancies when the banking agencies implement metadata changes in the CDR system whenever the Call Report forms or instructions are revised. Combining the two Call Report forms into a single form is not intended to increase the amount of data that any bank is currently required to report each quarter. In June 2010, the task force shared a draft combined form with the banking agencies' Call Report data users and analysts, and solicited their input on implementation issues that may arise from the introduction of a single form. Feedback on the implications of this change for downstream agency systems and UBPR ratios led the task force to defer combining the two forms into one form to a date beyond March 2011. The task force's options for moving forward on this project are also affected by the proposed migration of savings associations from the TFR to the Call Report in March 2012.

The task force conducted monthly interagency conference calls during 2010 to discuss Call Report instructional matters and related accounting issues to reach uniform interagency positions on these issues.

Central Data Repository

During 2010, the agencies continued to devote significant staff resources to enhance the CDR for processing the quarterly bank Call Reports and the UBPR.

The agencies' work during the first quarter was dedicated primarily to the tasks associated with completing the implementation of the UBPR within the CDR. The CDR became the system of record for the UBPR on March 29, 2010. In conjunction with the Task Force on Surveillance Systems, the banking agencies now process and distribute the UBPR using the interagency CDR Public Data Distribution website. In addition, the agencies implemented a major CDR enhancement release in December 2010. The December release provided enhancements

to improve Call Report processing, public data distribution, and UBPR processing.

Other Activities

In April 2010, the FDIC Board extended the Transaction Account Guarantee (TAG) Program from June 30 to December 31, 2010. The FDIC Board also changed the basis for calculating assessments beginning in the third quarter of 2010 from quarter-end to daily average balances. This necessitated a change in the TAG Program assessment data collected in the Call Report, the TFR, and the Report of Assets and Liabilities of U.S. Branches and Agencies of Foreign Banks (FFIEC 002 report) from those FDIC-insured institutions electing to participate in the program extension. Following task force approvals, the banking agencies and the OTS jointly published initial and final PRA *Federal Register* notices requesting comment on the proposed basis of reporting TAG Program data in these three reports in May and August 2010, respectively. OMB approved this reporting change in September 2010.

Section 343 of the Dodd-Frank Act amended the Federal Deposit Insurance Act to provide temporary unlimited insurance coverage to noninterest-bearing transaction accounts at all FDIC-insured institutions. This insurance coverage is in effect from December 31, 2010, through December 31, 2012, and replaces the FDIC's TAG Program. To support its administration of the Deposit Insurance Fund in response to Section 343, the FDIC determined that each insured institution should report the quarter-end dollar amount and number of noninterest-bearing transaction accounts (as defined in the Dodd-Frank Act) of more

than $250,000 beginning December 31, 2010. Following task force approvals, the banking agencies and the OTS jointly published initial and final PRA *Federal Register* notices requesting comment on the proposed collection of this information in the Call Report, the TFR, and the FFIEC 002 report in September and November 2010, respectively. OMB approved this reporting change in December 2010.

In August 2010, the task force approved, and the FRB published on behalf of the banking agencies, an initial PRA *Federal Register* notice requesting comment on proposed revisions to the FFIEC 002 report that would take effect in March 2011. These revisions incorporate several recent bank Call Report revisions into the FFIEC 002 report: additional detail on trading assets, changes to the reporting of certain time deposits, and additional detail and modified criteria for reporting on assets and liabilities measured at fair value. One comment was received supporting the proposed revisions. Following task force approval, the FRB published a final PRA *Federal Register* notice in January 2011. OMB approval of the FFIEC 002 reporting changes is pending.

In September 2010, an interagency group of subject matter experts on Basel II data collection recommended a limited number of revisions to the Advanced Capital Adequacy Framework Regulatory Reporting Requirements (FFIEC 101 report). These changes to the report, which would be implemented in March 2011, would merge the separate banking organization and savings association schedules for calculating total capital, segregate the reporting by bank holding companies of certain restricted core capital elements from other core capital elements, and streamline the reporting of equity exposures. In October 2010, the task force approved and the agencies published an initial PRA *Federal Register* notice requesting comment on these proposed revisions and an extension for three years of the agencies' authority to collect the FFIEC 101 report. No comments were received on the proposal. Following task force approval, the agencies published a final PRA *Federal Register* notice for the FFIEC 101 report in January 2011. Approval by OMB is pending.

Task Force on Supervision

The Task Force on Supervision coordinates and oversees matters relating to safety-and-soundness supervision and examination of depository institutions. It provides a forum for the member agencies and State Liaison Committee to promote quality, consistency, and effectiveness in examination and supervisory practices. While significant issues are referred, with recommendations, to the Council for action, the Council has delegated to the task force the authority to make certain decisions and recommendations, provided all task force members agree. Meetings are held regularly to address and resolve common supervisory issues. The task force has also established and maintains supervisory communication protocols to be used in emergencies. These protocols are periodically tested through table-top exercises with task force members and key supervisory personnel.

The task force has two subcommittees and a standing working group:

Task Force on Supervision meeting.

- The *Capital Subcommittee* serves as a forum for senior policy staff members to discuss various initiatives pertaining to the agencies' regulatory capital standards.

- The *Information Technology (IT) Subcommittee* serves as a forum to address information systems and technology policy issues as they relate to financial institutions. The IT Subcommittee oversees and administers the FFIEC member agencies' Technology Service Provider (TSP) Examination and Shared Application Software Review (SASR) programs. Through the FFIEC'S Multi-Regional Data Processing Servicer program, the agencies conduct joint information technology examinations of the largest, systemically important technology service providers and other entities that provide critical banking services. The SASR program provides a mechanism for the agencies to review and share information on mission-critical software applications, such as loans, deposits, general

ledger systems, and other critical software tools that are used by a large number of financial institutions. These programs help the agencies identify potential systemic risks and provide examiners with information that can reduce time and resources needed to examine the IT-related processing software and external services at user financial institutions.

- The *Bank Secrecy Act/Anti-Money Laundering (BSA/AML) Working Group* seeks to enhance coordination of BSA/AML training, guidance, and policy. The coordination includes continuing communication between federal and state banking agencies and the Financial Crimes Enforcement Network. The BSA/AML Working Group builds on existing efforts and works to strengthen the activities that are already being pursued by other formal and informal interagency groups providing oversight of various BSA/AML matters. BSA/AML training, guidance, and policy includes: (1) procedures and resource materials for examination purposes; (2) joint examiner training related to the FFIEC's BSA/AML Examination Manual; (3) outreach to the banking industry on BSA/AML policy matters; and (4) other issues related to consistency of BSA/AML supervision.

The task force also establishes ad hoc working groups to handle individual projects and assignments, as needed.

Initiatives Addressed in 2010

SAFE Act

A task force working group, together with the Farm Credit Administration (FCA), continued to coordinate efforts among the FFIEC agencies to implement provisions of the Secure and Fair Enforcement for Mortgage Licensing Act of 2008 (the Act). As required by the Act, mortgage loan originators (MLOs) employed by institutions that are regulated by a federal banking agency or the FCA must register with the Nationwide Mortgage Licensing System and Registry (NMLSR), obtain a unique identifier and maintain this registration. As envisioned, the NMLSR will improve the flow of information to and between regulators, providing increased accountability and tracking of MLOs, enhancing consumer protections, and providing consumer access to certain information on MLOs. In July 2010, the FFIEC agencies and the FCA issued the final rule to implement the requirements of the SAFE Act, with an effective date of October 1, 2010.

Enhanced Risk Management Practices

Current financial market and economic conditions present significant risk management challenges to institutions of all sizes. In this challenging environment, the task force established working groups to prepare the following issuances, which serve to reaffirm supervisory expectations for sound risk management practices by federal financial institutions:

- On January 7, 2010, the FFIEC released an advisory, adopted by the agencies, on sound interest rate risk (IRR) management practices for depository institutions. The advisory emphasizes the importance of effective corporate governance, policies and procedures, risk measuring and monitoring systems, stress testing, and internal controls related to the IRR exposures of institutions. It also clarifies various elements of existing guidance and describes selected IRR management techniques used by effective risk managers.

- On March 17, 2010 the FFIEC member agencies, in conjunction with Conference of State Bank Supervisors (CSBS) published final guidance on sound funding and liquidity risk management practices. The guidance summarizes the principles of sound liquidity risk management issued previously by the agencies and, when appropriate, supplements them with the "Principles for Sound Liquidity Risk Management and Supervision" issued in September 2008 by the Basel Committee on Banking Supervision.

- On June 7, 2010, an interagency policy statement on business combinations and FDIC- and NCUA-assisted transactions was issued that addresses the agencies' supervisory expectations and licensing considerations for financial institutions engaged in assisted acquisitions and bargain purchase transactions, as well as certain accounting and regulatory reporting requirements for business combinations.

- On April 30, 2010 the OCC, OTS, FRB, and FDIC issued final guidance to address the concentration risk attendant to correspondent banking relationships by managing the credit and funding risk associated with large exposures to correspondent counterparties.

- On December 2, 2010, interagency appraisal and evaluation guidelines were issued that update and clarify the agencies' minimum regulatory standards for appraisals. The guidelines emphasize that financial institutions are responsible for selecting appraisers and people performing evaluations based on their competence, experience, and knowledge of the market and type of property being valued. The guidelines also address advancements in information technology used in collateral valuation practices, and clarify standards for the industry's appropriate use of analytical methods and technological tools in developing evaluations.

Information Technology

Financial institutions' significant use of information technology services, whether generated internally or obtained from third-party service providers, contributes to their operational risk environment in general and their data security risk in particular. A major effort of the Information Technology Subcommittee (Subcommittee) and agencies is maintaining the FFIEC Information Technology Examination Handbook. The handbook consists of a series of topical booklets addressing issues such as business continuity planning, information security, and electronic banking. In 2010, the FFIEC published an update of the Retail Payment Systems Booklet. The booklet provides guidance to examiners, institutions, and technology service providers on identifying and controlling risks associated with retail payment systems and related activities. During the year, the Subcommittee devoted resources to enhancing the FFIEC's InfoBase so that updates to sections that are common to more than one handbook could be more efficiently updated.

The Subcommittee, in conjunction with the Task Force on Examiner Education, sponsors an annual Information Technology conference for the agencies' examination staff on emerging risks and industry best practices. The Subcommittee is also responsible for the coordination of the Multiregional Data Processing Servicer (MDPS) Program Oversight, which is ongoing. The FFIEC member agencies examine MDPS organizations because these entities pose a systemic risk to the banking system should one or more have operational or financial problems or fail. Since these companies service banks, thrifts, and credit unions, the FFIEC member agencies conduct interagency examinations of these large technology service providers. Interagency examinations provide a single examination report for the service providers. In February 2010 the Subcommittee held a supervisory strategy meeting with interagency examination teams from each MDPS to approve the examination strategies and schedules. The meeting also included a roundtable discussion among ITS principals and senior management from some of the MDPS companies.

The FFIEC member agencies completed examiner training via a webinar in March 2010 on the

Shared Application Software Review (SASR) Program designed to provide a uniform report on widely used software applications to the agencies and non-information technology examiners who examine banks using these software applications. The uniform report was revised in 2009 to enhance the efficiency of the review process for the original SASR program approved by the task force in 1990.

Capital Standards

Although each of the four federal banking agencies has its own capital regulations, the task force's standing Capital Subcommittee and several of its working groups promote joint issuance of capital rules and related interpretive guidance, thereby minimizing interagency differences and reducing the potential burden on the banking industry. The federal banking agencies have been re-examining our capital adequacy framework in light of the recent financial stress.

BSA/AML Working Group

The BSA/AML Working Group completed revisions to the BSA/AML Examination Manual (Manual) and examination procedures. The agencies released the Manual on April 29, 2010.

The BSA/AML working group sponsored its fourth FFIEC Advanced BSA/AML Specialists Conference in July 2010. Feedback from the conference was positive. The agencies continued to share information with the Financial Crimes Enforcement Network and with the Office of Foreign Assets Control.

Task Force on Surveillance Systems

The Task Force on Surveillance

Systems oversees the development and implementation of uniform interagency surveillance and monitoring systems. It provides a forum for the member agencies to discuss best practices to be used in those systems and to consider the development of new financial analysis tools. The task force's principal objective has been to develop and produce the Uniform Bank Performance Report (UBPR). UBPRs present financial data and peer group statistics of individual banks for current and historical periods. These reports are important tools for completing supervisory evaluations of a bank's condition and performance, as well as for planning onsite examinations. The banking agencies also use the data from these reports in their automated monitoring systems to identify potential or emerging problems in insured banks.

A UBPR is produced for each commercial bank and insured savings bank in the United States that is supervised by the Federal Reserve Board, the Federal Deposit Insurance Corporation, or the Office of the Comptroller of the Currency. UBPR data are also available to all state bank supervisors. While the UBPR is principally designed to meet the examination and surveillance needs of the federal and state banking agencies, the task force also makes the UBPR available to banks and the public through a public website, www.ffiec.gov/UBPR.htm.

Initiatives Addressed in 2010

Enhanced the Delivery of UBPR Data

The task force approved conversion of UBPR data processing and delivery to a completely new system in the FFIEC Central Data Repository (CDR). The multi-year

Task Force on Surveillance Systems meeting.

project included extensive analysis and testing during 2010 before approval as the system of record for UBPR data. Bankers, bank supervisors, and the general public have available many improvements to the UBPR including:

- Nightly updating of UBPR data

- Next day availability of UBPR report when a Call Report is filed

- View, print, and download all reports

- Custom Peer Group Tool can deliver a re-computed report in seconds

- Download all UBPR data in delimited files at no charge

- Standardized format for all reports

- Retention of all quarterly UBPR data beginning December 2001

- Expanded state-based peer group analysis

Improved UBPR Analysis of Deposits

Ratios that analyze brokered deposits as well as core and non-core deposits were revised to utilize new detail reported in the March 31, 2010 Call Report Schedule RE-E. New data reported included information on brokered deposits and large time deposits. Ratios found on the UBPR Page 4 Balance Sheet $, UBPR Page 6 Balance Sheet %, and UBPR Page 10 Liquidity and Investment Portfolio were affected.

Improved UBPR Analysis of Off-balance Sheet Activities

Ratios that analyze off-balance sheet activities found on UBPR Page 5 Off Balance Sheet Items were revised to utilize new information on commitments on 1–4 family mortgages and other loans found in Call Report Sched-

ule RC-L beginning March 31, 2010.

Improved UBPR Analysis of Loans

Ratios that analyze loan mix and concentrations found on UBPR Page 7A Analysis of Credit Allowance and Loan Mix and UBPR Page 7B Analysis of Concentrations of Credit were revised to utilize new information reported on loans to non-depository financial institutions and other loans on Call Report Schedule RC-C beginning March 31, 2010.

UBPR Delivered to a Wide Audience

UBPR for December 31, 2009; March 31, 2010; June 30, 2010; and September 30, 2010 were produced and delivered during 2010 to federal and state banking agencies. Additionally, the UBPR website was utilized to deliver the same data to bankers and the general public. The task force strives to deliver the most up-to-date UBPR data to all users. Thus current and historic UBPR data is updated nightly. Frequent updating allows the UBPR to remain synchronized with new Call Report data as it is being submitted by banks.

Projects Planned for 2011

- *Liquidity and funding*—The task force approved a working group to review UBPR treatment of liquidity measures, core and non-core funding and overall funding analysis. The review will include all Call Report changes planned for 2011.

- *Fiduciary activities*—The task force approved a working group to review the UBPR treatment of fiduciary data obtained from Call Schedule RC-T. This will be the first comprehensive review of this information since implementation in 2002 and will encompass new data collected in the 2009 Call Report.

- *Improved documentation of UBPR ratios*—The task force is undertaking a complete rewrite of the UBPR Users Guide. The review will re-focus the guide as a technical reference manual to provide Call Report based explanations of UBPR ratios. The guide will also offer high level explanations and define peer groups, peer group computations, and related elements as well.

- *Government guaranteed loans*— The task force will implement new ratios on UBPR Page 8 Analysis of Past Due, Nonaccrual & Restructured and UBPR Page 8A Analysis of Past Due, Nonaccrual & Restructured that will analyze the impact of government guarantees on past due loans. Along with ratios the UBPR will display associated peer group averages and percentile rankings. The data will be calculated for all historic quarters in the CDR.

Information Available on the UBPR Website

UBPR Availability

To provide broad banking industry and public access to information about the financial condition of insured banks, the task force publishes UBPR data for each institution shortly after the underlying Call Report is filed in the CDR. The UBPR is frequently refreshed to reflect amendments to underlying Call Report data and to incorporate any content-based changes agreed to by the task force. The on-line UBPR is a dynamic report that is closely synchronized with the underlying Call Report.

Other UBPR Reports

Several web-based statistical reports supporting UBPR analysis are also available and are updated nightly on the website. These reports (1) summarize the performance of all UBPR peer groups (determined by size, location, and business line), (2) detail the distribution of UBPR performance ratios for banks in each of these peer groups, (3) list the individual banks included in each peer group, and (4) compare a bank to the performance of a user-defined custom peer group.

Custom Peer Group Tool

The Custom Peer Group Tool allows bankers, bank supervisors, and the general public to create custom peer groups based on financial and geographical criteria. The tool can then display all UBPR pages with peer group statistics and percentile rankings derived from the custom peer group. The Custom Peer Group Tool can re-compute the entire UBPR using a custom peer group of up to 2,000 banks and deliver the results usually within seconds.

Bulk Data Download

The UBPR database within the CDR containing all data appearing on report pages for all banks may be downloaded as either a delimited file or in XBRL format. There is no charge for this service and downloads are typically fast.

Please visit www.ffiec.gov/UBPR. htm for additional information about the UBPR, including status, descriptions of pending changes, and the UBPR Users Guide. The site also provides access to the reports described above. For questions about the UBPR contact support by calling 1-888-237-3111, emailing cdr.help@ffiec.gov, or writing the Council at:

Federal Financial Institutions Examination Council
3501 Fairfax Drive, Room B7081a
Arlington, VA 22226-3550

THE FEDERAL FINANCIAL INSTITUTION REGULATORY AGENCIES AND THEIR SUPERVISED INSTITUTIONS

The five federal financial institution regulatory agencies represented on the Council have primary federal supervisory jurisdiction over 15,218 domestically chartered banks, thrift institutions, and credit unions. On December 31, 2010, these financial institutions held total assets of more than $16.1trillion. The Board of Governors of the Federal Reserve System and the Office of Thrift Supervision also have primary federal supervisory responsibility for commercial bank holding companies and for savings and loan holding companies, respectively.

Three banking agencies on the Council have authority to oversee the operations of U.S. branches and agencies of foreign banks. The International Banking Act of 1978 (IBA) authorizes the Office of the Comptroller of the Currency to license federal branches and agencies of foreign banks and permits U.S. branches that accept only wholesale deposits to apply for insurance with the Federal Deposit Insurance Corporation. According to the Federal Deposit Insurance Corporation Improvement Act of 1991 (FDICIA), foreign banks that wish to operate insured entities in the United States and accept retail deposits must organize under separate U.S. charters. Existing insured retail branches may continue to operate as branches. The IBA also subjects those U.S. offices of foreign banks to many provisions of the Federal Reserve Act and the Bank Holding Company Act. The IBA gives primary examining authority to the Office of the Comptroller of the Currency, the Federal Deposit Insurance Corporation, and various state authorities for the offices within their jurisdictions. The IBA also gives the Board of Governors of the Federal Reserve System residual examining authority over all U.S. banking operations of foreign banks.

Board of Governors of the Federal Reserve System

The Federal Reserve Board was established in 1913. It is headed by a seven-member Board of Governors; each member is appointed by the President, with the advice and consent of the Senate, for a fourteen-year term. Subject to confirmation by the Senate, the President selects one Board member to serve a four-year term as Chairperson and two members to serve as Vice Chairs; one serves in the absence of the Chairperson and the other is designated as Vice Chair for Supervision. The Federal Reserve Board's activities most relevant to the work of the Council are the following:

- overseeing the quality and efficiency of Reserve Bank examinations and supervision; monitoring of the financial condition, operations, and systemic risk of state member banks (i.e. state-chartered banks that are members of the Federal Reserve System), bank holding companies (BHCs) (including financial holding companies (FHCs)),[1] Edge Act and agreement corporations, and, in conjunction with the licensing authorities, carrying its authority to supervise and regulate the international operations of banking organizations headquartered in the United States, as well as the domestic activities of foreign banking organizations;

- developing, issuing, implementing, and communicating regulations, supervisory policies and guidance, and taking appropriate enforcement actions applicable to those organizations that are within the Federal Reserve Board's supervisory oversight authority; and

- approving or denying applications for mergers, acquisitions, and changes in control by state member banks and BHCs (including FHCs), applications for foreign operations of member banks and Edge Act and agreement corporations, and applications by foreign banks to establish or acquire U.S. banks and to establish U.S. branches, agencies, or representative offices.

Other supervisory and regulatory responsibilities of the Federal Reserve Board include regulating margin requirements on securities transactions, implementing certain statutes that protect consumers in credit and deposit transactions, monitoring compliance with other statutes (e.g. the money-laundering provisions of the Bank Secrecy Act), and regulating transactions between banking affiliates.

Policy decisions are implemented by the Federal Reserve Board or under delegated authority to the Director for the Division of Banking Supervision and Regulation and to the twelve Federal Reserve Banks—each of which has operational responsibility within a specific geographical area. The Reserve Bank Districts are headquartered in Boston, New York, Philadelphia, Cleveland, Richmond, Atlanta, Chicago, St. Louis, Minneapolis, Kansas City, Dallas, and San Francisco. Each Reserve

---

1. The Federal Reserve Board's role as the supervisor of a BHC or FHC is to review and assess the consolidated organization's operations, risk-management systems, and capital adequacy to ensure that the holding company and its non-bank subsidiaries do not threaten the viability of the company's depository institutions. In this role, the Federal Reserve Board serves as the "umbrella supervisor" of the consolidated organization. In fulfilling this role, the Federal Reserve Board relies to the fullest extent possible on information and analysis provided by the appropriate supervisory authority of the company's bank, securities, or insurance subsidiaries.

Bank has a president (chief executive officer) who serves for 5 years and is appointed by the bank's class B and class C directors, and other executive officers who report directly to the president. Among other responsibilities, a Reserve Bank employs a staff of examiners —who examine state member banks and Edge Act and agreement corporations, conduct BHC inspections, and examine the international operations of foreign banks—whose head offices are usually located within the Reserve Bank's District. When appropriate, examiners also visit the overseas offices of U.S. banking organizations to obtain financial and operating information to evaluate adherence to safe and sound banking practices.

National banks, which must be members of the Federal Reserve System, are chartered, regulated, and supervised by the Office of the Comptroller of the Currency. State-chartered banks may apply to and be accepted for membership in the Federal Reserve System, after which they are subject to the supervision and regulation of the Federal Reserve Board, which is coordinated with the state's banking authority. Insured state-chartered banks that are not members of the Federal Reserve System are regulated and supervised by the Federal Deposit Insurance Corporation. The Federal Reserve Board also has overall responsibil-ity for foreign banking operations, including both U.S. banks operating abroad and foreign banks operating branches within the United States.

On July 21, 2010, the President signed the financial regulatory reform bill (the Dodd-Frank Wall Street Reform and Consumer Protection Act (the Dodd-Frank Act)).[2] The Dodd-Frank Act gives the Federal Reserve Board new responsibilities including:

1. Membership in the newly formed Financial Stability Oversight Council (FSOC). The FSOC's responsibilities include identifying risks to financial stability and promoting market discipline. The FSOC has 10 designated voting members and 5 designated nonvoting advisory members.

2. Supervision of nonbank financial firms that are designated as systemically important by the FSOC.

3. Supervision and regulation of savings and loan holding companies (SLHCs).

2. Public Law No. 111-203, 124 Stat. 1376 (2010). Most provisions of the Dodd-Frank Act have general effective dates that are either effective on (1) the "transfer date" of the Office of Thrift Supervision, which is one-year after the date of enactment (July 21, 2011), or (2) one day after the date of enactment (July 22, 2010), unless otherwise specifically stated in the Act.

4. Development of enhanced prudential standards for large BHCs with $50 billion or more in assets, and systemically significant FSOC-designated non-bank financial firms (including requirements relating to capital, liquidity, stress tests, risk management, concentration limits, and credit exposure reporting).

Additionally, the Dodd-Frank Act created an independent Consumer Financial Protection Bureau, housed within the Federal Reserve Board, and charged with administering the consumer financial protection laws.

The Federal Reserve Board covers the expenses of its operations with revenue it generates principally from assessments on the twelve Federal Reserve Banks. The Dodd-Frank Act directs the Federal Reserve Board to collect assessments, fees, and other charges that are equal to the expenses incurred by the Federal Reserve to carry out its responsibilities with respect to: (1) BHCs and SLHCs with assets equal to or greater than $50 billion; and (2) all non-bank financial companies supervised by the Federal Reserve Board.[3]

3. The effective date is one-year after the date of the Dodd-Frank Act's enactment.

Federal Deposit Insurance Corporation

Congress created the Federal Deposit Insurance Corporation (FDIC) in 1933 with a mission to insure bank deposits and reduce the economic disruptions caused by bank failures. Management of the FDIC is vested in a five-member Board of Directors. No more than three board members may be of the same political party. Three of the directors are directly appointed by the President, with the advice and consent of the Senate, for six-year terms. One of the three directors is designated by the President as Chairman for a term of five years, and another is designated as Vice Chairman. The other two Board members are the Comptroller of the Currency and the Director of the Office of Thrift Supervision. In 2011, pursuant to the Dodd-Frank Wall Street Reform and Consumer Protection Act of 2010 (the Dodd-Frank Act), the Chairman of the Consumer Financial Protection Bureau will be added to the FDIC Board of Directors and replace the Director of the Office of Thrift Supervision.

The FDIC insures deposits at all insured commercial banks and savings institutions. On October 3, 2008, the Emergency Economic Stabilization Act of 2008 was approved, temporarily raising the standard maximum deposit insurance amount (SMDIA) on federal deposit insurance coverage from $100,000 to $250,000 per depositor through December 31, 2009. On May 20, 2009, the Helping Families Save Their Homes Act was approved, extending the SMDIA temporary increase to $250,000 per depositor through December 31, 2013. On July 22, 2010, the Dodd-Frank Act made permanent the increase to $250,000 of the SMDIA.

On November 9, 2010, the FDIC Board of Directors issued a final rule to implement Section 343 of the Dodd-Frank Act to provide temporary unlimited deposit insurance coverage for noninterest-bearing transaction accounts at all FDIC-insured depository institutions. The separate coverage for noninterest-bearing transaction accounts became effective on December 31, 2010 and terminates on December 31, 2012. In issuing the November Final Rule, the FDIC Board confirmed it would not extend the FDIC's Transaction Account Guarantee Program implemented on October 14, 2008, beyond its sunset date of December 31, 2010. On December 29, 2010, President Obama signed into law an amendment to the Federal Deposit Insurance Act to include Interest on Lawyer Trust Accounts (IOLTAs) within the definition of noninterest-bearing transaction accounts. As a result, IOLTAs will receive temporary unlimited insurance coverage at all FDIC-insured institutions from December 31, 2010 through December 31, 2012.

Any depository institution that receives deposits may be insured by the FDIC after application to and examination and approval by the FDIC. After considering the (1) applicant's financial history and condition, (2) adequacy of the capital structure, (3) future earnings prospects, (4) general character of the management, (5) risk presented to the insurance fund, (6) convenience and needs of the community to be served, and (7) consistency of corporate powers, the FDIC may approve or deny an application for insurance. The Federal Deposit Insurance Corporation Improvement Act of 1991 (FDICIA) expanded the FDIC's approval authority to include national banks, all state-chartered banks that are members of the Federal Reserve System, and federal and state-chartered savings associations.

The FDIC has primary federal regulatory and supervisory authority over insured state-chartered banks that are not members of the Federal Reserve System, and it has the authority to examine for insurance purposes any insured financial institution, either directly or in cooperation with state or other federal supervisory authorities. The FDICIA gives the FDIC backup enforcement authority over all insured institutions; that is, the FDIC can recommend that the appropriate federal agency take action against an insured institution and may do so itself if deemed necessary. In addition, the Dodd-Frank Act expanded the FDIC's authority to manage the failure of systemically significant firms.

The FDIC's supervisory activities are conducted by the Division of Supervision and Consumer Protection. The division is organized into six regional offices and two area offices. The regional offices are located in Atlanta, Chicago, Dallas, Kansas City, New York, and San Francisco. The two area offices are located in Boston (reports to New York) and Memphis (reports to Dallas). In addition to the regional and area offices, the FDIC maintains eighty-five field territory offices for risk management and seventy-four field territory offices for compliance, with dedicated examiners assigned to many of the largest financial institutions.

Bank liquidations are handled by the Division of Resolutions and Receiverships. In protecting insured deposits, the FDIC is charged with resolving the problems of insured failed depository institutions at the least possible cost to the deposit insurance fund. In carrying out this responsibility, the FDIC engages in several activities, including paying off deposits, arranging the purchase of assets and assumption of liabilities of failed institutions, effecting insured deposit transfers between institutions, creating and operating temporary bridge banks until a resolution can be accomplished, and using its conservatorship powers.

In response to the changing risk profile of the Corporation and the industry, and to meet certain mandates in the Dodd-Frank Act, the FDIC initiated various structural changes in 2010, including the creation of four new organizations.

The Office of Complex Financial Institutions will oversee the orderly liquidation of bank holding companies with more than $100 billion in assets as well as significant non-bank financial companies, as determined by the new Financial Stability Oversight Council, that fail.

The Division of Depositor and Consumer Protection will provide increased visibility to the FDIC's compliance examination and enforcement program for thousands of community banks with $10 billion or less in total assets.

The Office of Corporate Risk Management will strategically manage a comprehensive program that addresses the Corporation's emerging and crisis related risks.

The Office of Minority and Women Inclusion will be responsible for all matters of the agency relating to diversity in management, employment and business activities.

National Credit Union Administration

The National Credit Union Administration, established by the Federal Credit Union Act (Section 1752a) of Congress in 1934, is the agency that supervises the nation's federal credit union system. A three-member bipartisan board appointed by the President for six-year terms manages the National Credit Union Administration. The President also selects a member to serve as Chair of the board.

The main responsibilities of the National Credit Union Administration are the following:

- charter, examine, and supervise more than 4,600 federal credit unions nationwide;

- administer the National Credit Union Share Insurance Fund (NCUSIF), which insures member share accounts in more than 7,400 U.S. federal and state-chartered credit unions;

- administer the Temporary Corporate Credit Union Stabiliza-

tion Fund, a borrowing facility and assessment authority for corporate credit union issues; and

- manage the Central Liquidity Facility, a central bank for credit unions, which provides liquidity to the credit union system.

The National Credit Union Administration also has statutory authority to examine and supervise NCUSIF-insured, state-chartered credit unions in coordination with state agencies.

The National Credit Union Administration has five regional offices across the United States that administers its responsibility to charter and supervise credit unions. Its examiners conduct on-site examinations and supervision of each federal credit union and selected state-chartered credit unions. The National Credit Union Administration is funded by the credit unions it regulates and insures.

Office of the Comptroller of the Currency

The Office of the Comptroller of the Currency (OCC) is the oldest federal bank regulatory agency, established as a bureau of the Treasury Department by the National Currency Act of 1863. It is headed by the Comptroller of the Currency, who is appointed to a five-year term by the President with the advice and consent of the Senate. The Comptroller is also a Director of the FDIC and a Director of the Neighborhood Reinvestment Corporation.

The OCC was created by Congress to charter, regulate, and supervise national banks. The OCC regulates and supervises 1,451 national banks and trust companies and 51 federal branches of foreign banks accounting for approximately 70 percent of the total assets of all U.S. commercial banks and branches of foreign banks. In 2011, pursuant to the Dodd-Frank Wall Street Reform and Consumer Protection Act, the OCC will assume supervisory responsibility for federal savings associations, as well as rulemaking authority relating to all savings associations.

The OCC seeks to ensure that national banks soundly manage their risks, comply with applicable laws, compete effectively with other providers of financial services, offer products and services that meet the needs of customers, and provide fair access to financial services and fair treatment of their customers. The OCC's mission-critical programs include:

- Chartering national banks and issuing interpretations related to permissible banking activities.

- Establishing and communicating regulations, policies, and operating guidance applicable to national banks.

- Supervising the national banking system through on-site examinations, off-site monitoring, systemic risk analyses, and appropriate enforcement activities.

To meet its objectives, the OCC maintains a nationwide staff of bank examiners and other professional and support personnel. Headquartered in Washington, D.C., the OCC has four district offices in Chicago, Dallas, Denver, and New York. In addition, the OCC maintains a network of 49 field offices and 22 satellite locations in cities throughout the United States, as well as resident examiner teams in 18 of the largest national banking companies and an examining office in London, England.

The Comptroller receives advice on policy and operational issues from an Executive Committee, comprised of senior agency officials who lead major business units.

The OCC is funded primarily by semiannual assessments on national banks, interest revenue from its investment in U.S. Treasury securities, and other fees. The OCC does not receive congressional appropriations for any of its operations.

Office of Thrift Supervision

The Office of Thrift Supervision was established as a bureau of the U. S. Department of the Treasury in 1989. The Office of Thrift Supervision charters and is the primary regulator for all federal savings associations, and shares joint responsibility with state authorities for supervision of all state savings associations. The Office of Thrift Supervision is also the primary regulator for all savings and loan holding companies.

The mission of the Office of Thrift Supervision is to supervise savings associations and their holding companies in order to maintain their safety and soundness and compliance with consumer laws, and to encourage a competitive industry that meets America's financial service needs.

The Office of Thrift Supervision carries out its mission by (1) adopting regulations governing the thrift institution industry, (2) examining and supervising savings associations and their affiliates, (3) taking appropriate action to enforce compliance with federal laws and regulations, and (4) acting on applications to charter or acquire a savings association. The Office of Thrift Supervision also has the authority to regulate, examine, supervise, and take enforcement action against savings and loan holding companies and other affiliates, as well as entities that provide services to savings associations.

The Office of Thrift Supervision is headed by a Director appointed by the President, with the advice and consent of the Senate, to serve a five-year term. The Director determines policy for the Office of Thrift Supervision and makes final decisions on regulations governing the industry as a whole and on measures affecting individual institutions. The Director also serves as a Director of the Federal Deposit Insurance Corporation and as a Director of the Neighborhood Reinvestment Corporation.

The agency conducts its operations from its headquarters in Washington, D.C., and four regional offices located in Jersey City, New Jersey (Northeast Region); Atlanta, Georgia (Southeast Region); Chicago, Illinois (Central Region); and Dallas, Texas (Western Region).

The Office of Thrift Supervision uses no congressional appropriations to fund any of its operations. It draws its revenues primarily through fees and assessments levied on the institutions it regulates.

According to the provisions of the Dodd-Frank Wall Street Reform and Consumer Protection Act of 2010 (the Dodd-Frank Act) the Office of Thrift Supervision will be closed in July 2011. While most of its functions will be transferred to the Office of the Comptroller of the Currency, certain other authorities of the Office of Thrift Supervision will be transferred to the Federal Deposit Insurance Corporation and the Board of Governors of the Federal Reserve System.

ASSETS, LIABILITIES, AND NET WORTH of U.S. Commercial Banks, Thrift Institutions, and Credit Unions as of December 31, 2010[1]

Billions of dollars

Item	Total	U.S. Commercial Banks[2] National	State Member	State Non-Member	U.S. Branches and Agencies of Foreign Banks[3]	Thrift Institutions OTS-Regulated[4] Federal Charter	State Charter	Other FDIC-Supervised Savings Banks	Credit Unions[5] Federal Charter	State Charter
Total assets	*16,143*	*8,432*	*1,694*	*1,938*	*1,912*	*920*	*12*	*321*	*500*	*414*
Total loans and receivables (net)	8,185	4,274	833	1,269	475	563	8	205	303	255
Loans secured by real estate[6]	4,615	2,290	524	835	35	436	8	178	163	146
Consumer loans[7]	1,574	957	62	209	0	88	0	6	143	109
Commercial and industrial loans	1,431	751	182	191	236	50	0	15	2	4
All other loans and lease receivables[8]	805	439	89	65	203	0	0	9	0	0
LESS: Allowance for possible loan and lease losses	240	164	23	30	0	11	0	3	5	4
Federal funds sold and securities purchased under agreements to resell	547	415	21	17	87	4	0	2	0	1
Cash and due from depository institutions[9]	1,523	563	227	133	397	49	1	18	73	62
Securities and other obligations[10]	3,015	1,620	370	362	169	245	2	69	101	77
U.S. government obligations[11]	861	255	63	97	56	180	2	54	87	67
Obligations of state and local governments[12]	182	84	27	60	0	6	0	5	0	0
Other securities	1,971	1,282	279	204	113	59	0	10	14	10
Other assets[13]	2,873	1,560	243	158	783	59	1	27	23	19
Total liabilities	*14,538*	*7,494*	*1,491*	*1,714*	*1,912*	*812*	*10*	*283*	*449*	*373*
Total deposits and shares[14]	11,282	5,763	1,257	1,491	1,078	661	9	237	427	359
Federal funds purchased and securities sold under agreements to repurchase	823	419	69	40	247	38	0	10	0	0
Other borrowings[15]	1,504	814	93	157	280	99	1	32	18	10
Other liabilities[16]	928	497	72	26	307	14	0	3	4	4
Net worth[17]	*1,607*	*938*	*203*	*225*	*2*	*108*	*2*	*37*	*51*	*41*
Memorandum: Number of institutions reporting	15,218	1,381	817	4,316	233	670	61	398	4,589	2,750

Footnotes to Tables

1. The table covers institutions, including those in Puerto Rico and U.S. territories and possessions, insured by the Federal Deposit Insurance Corporation or National Credit Union Savings Insurance Fund. All branches and agencies of foreign banks in the United States, but excluding any in Puerto Rico and U.S. territories and possessions, are covered whether or not insured. Excludes Edge Act and agreement corporations that are not subsidiaries of U.S. commercial banks.

2. Reflects fully consolidated statements of FDIC-insured U.S. banks—including their foreign branches, foreign subsidiaries, branches in Puerto Rico and U.S. territories and possessions, and FDIC insured banks in Puerto Rico and U.S. territories and possessions. Excludes bank holding companies.

3. Data are for federally insured natural person credit unions only.

4. Data for thrift institutions regulated by the OTS reflects fully consolidated statements of condition and operations. Data for OTS regulated thrifts owned directly by other thrifts are excluded to avoid double counting results already included in the parents financial statements.

5. These institutions are not required to file reports of income.

6. Includes loans secured by residential property, commercial property, farmland (including improvements) and unimproved land; and construction loans secured by real estate.

7. Includes loans, except those secured by real estate, to individuals for household, family, and other personal expenditures including both installment and single payment loans. Net of unearned income on installment loans.

Notes continue on the next page

INCOME AND EXPENSES of U.S. Commercial Banks and Thrift Institutions for the Twelve Months Ending December 31, 2010[1]

Billions of dollars

Item	Total	U.S. Commercial Banks[2]			Thrift Institutions			Credit Unions[3]	
					OTS-Regulated[4]		Other FDIC-Super-vised Savings Banks		
		National	State Member	State Non-Member	Federal Charter	State Charter		Federal Charter	State Charter
Operating income	825	494	90	115	59	0	15	29	23
Interest and fees on loans	454	254	42	79	34	0	11	19	15
Other interest and dividend income	124	77	14	13	12	0	2	3	3
All other operating income	244	161	34	22	13	0	2	7	5
Operating expenses	702	408	82	104	48	0	13	26	21
Salaries and benefits	184	108	24	24	9	0	4	8	7
Interest on deposits and shares	77	31	8	18	8	0	3	5	4
Interest on other borrowed money	40	24	4	5	5	0	1	1	0
Provision for loan and lease losses	164	104	18	24	10	0	1	4	3
All other operating expenses	237	141	28	33	16	0	4	8	7
Net operating income	*123*	*86*	*8*	*11*	*11*	*0*	*2*	*3*	*2*
Securities gains and losses	9	6	1	2	0	0	0	0	0
Extraordinary Items	-1	-1	0	0	0	0	0	0	0
Income taxes	38	26	3	4	4	0	1	0	0
Net income	*93*	*65*	*6*	*8*	*7*	*0*	*2*	*3*	*2*
Memorandum: Number of institutions reporting	14,982	1,381	817	4,316	670	61	398	4,589	2,750

8. Includes loans to financial institutions, for purchasing or carrying securities, to finance agricultural production and other loans to farmers (except those secured by real estate), to states and political subdivisions and public authorities, and miscellaneous types of loans.

9. Includes vault cash, cash items in process of collection, and balances with U.S. and foreign banks and other depository institutions (including demand and time deposits and certificates of deposit for all categories of institutions).

10. Includes government and corporate securities, including mortgage-backed securities and obligations of states and political subdivisions and of U.S. government agencies and corporations.

11. U.S. Treasury securities and securities of, and loans to, U.S. government agencies and corporations.

12. Securities issued by states and political subdivisions and public authorities, except for savings and loan associations and U.S. branches and agencies of foreign banks that do not report these securities separately. Loans to states and political subdivisions and public authorities are included in "All other loans and lease receivables."

13. Customers' liabilities on acceptances, real property owned, various accrual accounts, and miscellaneous assets. For U.S. branches and agencies of foreign banks, also includes net due from head office and other related institutions. For SAIF-insured institutions, also includes equity investment in service corporation subsidiaries.

14. Includes demand, savings, and time deposits, (including certificates of deposit at commercial banks, U.S. branches and agencies of foreign banks, and savings banks), credit balances at U.S. agencies of foreign banks and share balances at savings and loan associations and credit unions (including certificates of deposit, NOW accounts, and share draft accounts). For U.S. commercial banks, includes deposits in foreign offices, branches in U.S. territories and possessions, and Edge Act and Agreement corporation subsidiaries.

15. Includes interest-bearing demand notes issued to the U.S. Treasury, borrowing from Federal Reserve Banks and Federal Home Loan Banks, subordinated debt, limited life preferred stock, and other nondeposit borrowing.

16. Includes depository institutions' own mortgage borrowing, liability for capitalized leases, liability on acceptances executed, various accrual accounts, and miscellaneous liabilities. For U.S. branches and agencies of foreign banks, also includes net owed to head office and other related institutions.

17. Includes capital stock, surplus, capital reserves, and undivided profits.

NOTE: Data are rounded to nearest billion. Consequently, some information may not reconcile precisely. Additionally, balances less than $500 million will show as zero.

APPENDIX A: RELEVANT STATUTES

Federal Financial Institutions Examination Council Act

12 U.S.C. § 3301. Declaration of purpose

It is the purpose of this chapter to establish a Financial Institutions Examination Council which shall prescribe uniform principles and standards for the Federal examination of financial institutions by the Office of the Comptroller of the Currency, the Federal Deposit Insurance Corporation, the Board of Governors of the Federal Reserve System, the Federal Home Loan Bank Board, and the National Credit Union Administration and make recommendations to promote uniformity in the supervision of these financial institutions. The Council's actions shall be designed to promote consistency in such examination and to insure progressive and vigilant supervision.

12 U.S.C. § 3302. Definitions

As used in this chapter—

(1) the term "Federal financial institutions regulatory agencies" means the Office of the Comptroller of the Currency, the Board of Governors of the Federal Reserve System, the Federal Deposit Insurance Corporation, the Office of Thrift Supervision, and the National Credit Union Administration;

(2) the term "Council" means the Financial Institutions Examination Council; and

(3) the term "financial institution" means a commercial bank, a savings bank, a trust company, a savings association, a building and loan association, a homestead association, a cooperative bank, or a credit union.

12 U.S.C. § 3303. Financial Institutions Examination Council

(a) Establishment; composition

There is established the Financial Institutions Examination Council which shall consist of—

(1) the Comptroller of the Currency,

(2) the Chairman of the Board of Directors of the Federal Deposit Insurance Corporation,

(3) a Governor of the Board of Governors of the Federal Reserve System designated by the Chairman of the Board,

(4) the ***Director of the Consumer Financial Protection Bureau***,[1]

(5) the Chairman of the National Credit Union Administration Board; and

(6) the Chairman of the State Liaison Committee

(b) Chairmanship

The members of the Council shall select the first chairman of the Council. Thereafter the chairmanship shall rotate among the members of the Council.

---

1. The Dodd Frank Wall Street Reform and Consumer Protection Act of 2010 amended several provisions in the relevant statutes, including excerpts contained in this appendix. Changes are shown as bolded and italicized. The amendments relating to the Consumer Financial Protection Bureau are not effective until the designated transfer date (currently July 21, 2011).

(c) Term of office

The term of the Chairman of the Council shall be two years.

(d) Designation of officers and employees

The members of the Council may, from time to time, designate other officers or employees of their respective agencies to carry out their duties on the Council.

(e) Compensation and expenses

Each member of the Council shall serve without additional compensation but shall be entitled to reasonable expenses incurred while carrying out his official duties as such a member.

12 U.S.C. § 3304. Costs and expenses of Council

One-fifth of the costs and expenses of the Council, including the salaries of its employees, shall be paid by each of the Federal financial institutions regulatory agencies. Annual assessments for such share shall be levied by the Council based upon its projected budget for the year, and additional assessments may be made during the year, if necessary.

12 U.S.C. § 3305. Functions of Council

(a) Establishment of principles and standards

The Council shall establish uniform principles and standards and report forms for the examination of financial institutions which shall be applied by the Federal financial institutions regulatory agencies.

(b) Making recommendations

regarding supervisory matters and adequacy of supervisory tools

(1) The Council shall make recommendations for uniformity in other supervisory matters, such as, but not limited to, classifying loans subject to country risk, identifying financial institutions in need of special supervisory attention, and evaluating the soundness of large loans that are shared by two or more financial institutions. In addition, the Council shall make recommendations regarding the adequacy of supervisory tools for determining the impact of holding company operations on the financial institutions within the holding company and shall consider the ability of supervisory agencies to discover possible fraud or questionable and illegal payments and practices which might occur in the operation of financial institutions or their holding companies.

(2) When a recommendation of the Council is found unacceptable by one or more of the applicable Federal financial institutions regulatory agencies, the agency or agencies shall submit to the Council, within a time period specified by the Council, a written statement of the reasons the recommendation is unacceptable.

(c) Development of uniform reporting system

The Council shall develop uniform reporting systems for federally supervised financial institutions, their holding companies, and non-financial institution subsidiaries of such institutions or holding companies. The authority to develop uniform reporting systems shall not restrict or amend the requirements of section 78l(i) of Title 15.

(d) Conducting schools for examiners and assistant examiners

The Council shall conduct schools for examiners and assistant examiners employed by the Federal financial institutions regulatory agencies. Such schools shall be open to enrollment by employees of State financial institutions supervisory agencies and employees of the Federal Housing Finance Board under conditions specified by the Council.

(e) Affect on Federal regulatory agency research and development of new financial institutions supervisory agencies

Nothing in this chapter shall be construed to limit or discourage Federal regulatory agency research and development of new financial institutions supervisory methods and tools, nor to preclude the field testing of any innovation devised by any Federal regulatory agency.

(f) Annual report

Not later than April 1 of each year, the Council shall prepare an annual report covering its activities during the preceding year.

(g) Flood insurance

The Council shall consult with and assist the Federal entities for lending regulation, as such term is defined in section 4121(a) of Title 42, in developing and coordinating uniform standards and requirements for use by regulated lending institutions under the national flood insurance program.

12 U.S.C. § 3306. State liaison

To encourage the application of uniform examination principles and standards by State and Federal supervisory agencies, the Council shall establish a liaison committee composed of five representatives of State agencies which supervise financial institutions which shall meet at least twice a year with the Council. Members of the liaison committee shall receive a reasonable allowance for necessary expenses incurred in attending meetings.

Members of the Liaison Committee shall elect a chairperson from among the members serving on the committee.

12 U.S.C. § 3307. Administration

(a) Authority of Chairman of Council

The Chairman of the Council is authorized to carry out and to delegate the authority to carry out the internal administration of the Council, including the appointment and supervision of employees and the distribution of business among members, employees, and administrative units.

(b) Use of personnel, services, and facilities of Federal financial institutions regulatory agencies, Federal Reserve banks, and Federal Home Loan Banks.

In addition to any other authority conferred upon it by this chapter, in carrying out its functions under this chapter, the Council may utilize, with their consent and to the extent practical, the personnel, services, and facilities of the Federal financial institutions regulatory agencies, Federal Reserve banks, and Federal Home Loan Banks, with or without reimbursement therefore.

(c) Compensation, authority, and duties of officers and employees; experts and consultants

In addition, the Council may—

(1) subject to the provisions of Title 5 relating to the competitive service, classification, and General Schedule pay rates, appoint and fix the compensation of such officers and employees as are necessary to

carry out the provisions of this chapter, and to prescribe the authority and duties of such officers and employees; and (2) obtain the services of such experts and consultants as are necessary to carry out the provisions of this chapter.

12 U.S.C. § 3308. Access to books, accounts, records, etc., by Council

For the purpose of carrying out this chapter, the Council shall have access to all books, accounts, records, reports, files, memorandums, papers, things, and property belonging to or in use by Federal financial institutions regulatory agencies, including reports of examination of financial institutions or their holding companies from whatever source, together with workpapers and correspondence files related to such reports, whether or not a part of the report, and all without any deletions.

12 U.S.C. § 3309. Risk management training

(a) Seminars

The Council shall develop and administer training seminars in risk management for its employees and the employees of insured financial institutions.

(b) Study of risk management training program

Not later than end of the 1-year period beginning on August 9, 1989, the Council shall—

(1) conduct a study on the feasibility and appropriateness of establishing a formalized risk management training program designed to lead to the certification of Risk Management Analysts; and

(2) report to the Congress the results of such study.

12 U.S.C. § 3310. Establishment of Appraisal Subcommittee

There shall be within the Council a subcommittee to be known as the "Appraisal Subcommittee," which shall consist of the designees of the heads of the Federal financial institutions regulatory agencies, the *Bureau of Consumer Financial Protection, and the Federal Housing Finance Agency*. Each such designee shall be a person who has demonstrated knowledge and competence concerning the appraisal profession. *At all times at least one member of the Appraisal Subcommittee shall have demonstrated knowledge and competence through licensure, certification, or professional designation within the appraisal profession.*

12 U.S.C. § 3311. Required review of regulations

(a) In general

Not less frequently than once every 10 years, the Council and each appropriate Federal banking agency represented on the Council shall conduct a review of all regulations prescribed by the Council or by any such appropriate Federal banking agency, respectively, in order to identify outdated or otherwise unnecessary regulatory requirements imposed on insured depository institutions.

(b) Process

In conducting the review under subsection (a) of this section, the Council or the appropriate Federal banking agency shall—

(1) categorize the regulations described in subsection (a) of this section by type (such as consumer regulations, safety and soundness regulations, or such other designations as determined by the Council, or the appropriate Federal banking agency); and

(2) at regular intervals, provide notice and solicit public comment on a particular category or categories of regulations, requesting commentators to identify areas of the regulations that are outdated, unnecessary, or unduly burdensome.

(c) Complete review

The Council or the appropriate Federal banking agency shall ensure that the notice and comment period described in subsection (b)(2) of this section is conducted with respect to all regulations described in subsection (a) of this section not less frequently than once every 10 years.

(d) Regulatory response

The Council or the appropriate Federal banking agency shall—

(1) publish in the Federal Register a summary of the comments received under this section, identifying significant issues raised and providing comment on such issues; and

(2) eliminate unnecessary regulations to the extent that such action is appropriate.

(e) Report to Congress

Not later than 30 days after carrying out subsection (d)(1) of this section, the Council shall submit to the Congress a report, which shall include—

(1) a summary of any significant issues raised by public comments received by the Council and the appropriate Federal banking agencies under this section and the relative merits of such issues; and

(2) an analysis of whether the appropriate Federal banking agency involved is able to address the regulatory burdens associated with such issues by regulation, or whether such bur-

dens must be addressed by legislative action.

Excerpts from Statute Governing Appraisal Subcommittee

12 U.S.C. § 3332. Functions of Appraisal Subcommittee

(a) In general

The Appraisal Subcommittee shall—

(1) monitor the requirements established by States—

(A) for the certification and licensing of individuals who are qualified to perform appraisals in connection with federally related transactions, including a code of professional responsibility; and

(B) for the registration and supervision of the operations and activities of an appraisal management company; and

(2) monitor the requirements established by the Federal financial institutions regulatory agencies with respect to—

(A) appraisal standards for federally related transactions under their jurisdiction, and

(B) determinations as to which federally related transactions under their jurisdiction require the services of a State certified appraiser and which require the services of a State licensed appraiser;

(3) maintain a national registry of State certified and licensed appraisers who are eligible to perform appraisals in federally related transactions; and

(4) Omitted.

(5) transmit an annual report to the Congress not later than June 15 of each year that describes the manner in which each function assigned to the Appraisal Subcommittee has been carried out during the preceding year. The report shall also detail the activities of the Appraisal Subcommittee, including the results of all audits of State appraiser regulatory agencies, and provide an accounting of disapproved actions and warnings taken in the previous year, including a description of the conditions causing the disapproval and actions taken to achieve compliance.

(6) maintain a national registry of appraisal management companies that either are registered with and subject to supervision of a State appraiser certifying and licensing agency or are operating subsidiaries of a Federally regulated financial institution.

(b) Monitoring and reviewing Foundation

The Appraisal Subcommittee shall monitor and review the practices, procedures, activities, and organizational structure of the Appraisal Foundation.

12 U.S.C. § 3333. Chairperson of Appraisal Subcommittee; term of Chairperson; meetings

(a) Chairperson

The Council shall select the Chairperson of the subcommittee. The term of the Chairperson shall be two years.

(b) Meetings; quorum; voting

The Appraisal Subcommittee shall *meet in public session after notice in the Federal Register, but may close certain portions of these meetings related to personnel and review of preliminary State audit reports,* at the call of the Chairperson or a majority of its members when there is business to be conducted. A majority of members of the Appraisal Subcommittee shall constitute a quorum but 2 or more members may hold hearings. Decisions of the Appraisal Subcommittee shall be made by the vote of a majority of its members. *The subject matter discussed in any closed or executive session shall be described in the Federal Register notice of the meeting.*

Excerpts from Home Mortgage Disclosure Act

12 U.S.C. § 2801. Congressional findings and declaration of purpose

(a) Findings of Congress

The Congress finds that some depository institutions have sometimes contributed to the decline of certain geographic areas by their failure pursuant to their chartering responsibilities to provide adequate home financing to qualified applicants on reasonable terms and conditions.

(b) Purpose of chapter

The purpose of this chapter is to provide the citizens and public officials of the United States with sufficient information to enable them to determine whether depository institutions are filling their obligations to serve the housing needs of the communities and neighborhoods in which they are located and to assist public officials in their determination of the distribution of public sector investments in a manner designed to improve the private investment environment.

(c) Construction of chapter

Nothing in this chapter is intended to, nor shall it be construed to, encourage unsound lending practices or the allocation of credit.

12 U.S.C. § 2803. Maintenance of records and public disclosure

(f) Data disclosure system; operation, etc.

The Federal Financial Institutions Examination Council, in consultation with the Secretary, shall implement a system to facilitate access to data required to be disclosed under this section. Such system shall include arrangements for a central depository of data in each primary metropolitan statistical area, metropolitan statistical area, or consolidated metropolitan statistical area that is not comprised of designated primary metropolitan statistical areas. Disclosure statements shall be made available to the public for inspection and copying at such central depository of data for all depository institutions which are required to disclose information under this section (or which are exempted pursuant to section 2805(b) of this title) and which have a home office or branch office within such primary metropolitan statistical area, metropolitan statistical area, or consolidated metropolitan statistical area that is not comprised of designated primary metropolitan statistical areas.

12 U.S.C. § 2809. Compilation of aggregate data

(a) Commencement; scope of data and tables

Beginning with data for calendar year 1980, the Federal Financial Institutions Examination Council shall compile each year, for each primary metropolitan statistical area, metropolitan statistical area, or consolidated metropolitan statistical area that is not comprised of designated primary metropolitan statistical areas, aggregate data by census tract for all depository institutions which are required to disclose data under section 2803 of

this title or which are exempt pursuant to section 2805(b) of this title. The Council shall also produce tables indicating, for each primary metropolitan statistical area, metropolitan statistical area, or consolidated metropolitan statistical area that is not comprised of designated primary metropolitan statistical areas, aggregate lending patterns for various categories of census tracts grouped according to location, age of housing stock, income level, and racial characteristics.

(b) Staff and data processing resources

The Board shall provide staff and data processing resources to the Council to enable it to carry out the provisions of subsection (a) of this section.

(c) Availability to public

The data and tables required pursuant to subsection (a) of this section shall be made available to the public no later than December 31 of the year following the calendar year on which the data is based.

Excerpts from S.A.F.E. Mortgage Licensing Act

12 U.S.C. § 5101. Purposes and methods for establishing a mortgage licensing system and registry

In order to increase uniformity, reduce regulatory burden, enhance consumer protection, and reduce fraud, the States, through the Conference of State Bank Supervisors and the American Association of Residential Mortgage Regulators, are hereby encouraged to establish a Nationwide Mortgage Licensing System and Registry for the residential mortgage industry that accomplishes all of the following objectives:

(1) Provides uniform license applications and reporting

requirements for State-licensed loan originators.

(2) Provides a comprehensive licensing and supervisory database.

(3) Aggregates and improves the flow of information to and between regulators.

(4) Provides increased accountability and tracking of loan originators.

(5) Streamlines the licensing process and reduces the regulatory burden.

(6) Enhances consumer protections and supports anti-fraud measures.

(7) Provides consumers with easily accessible information, offered at no charge, utilizing electronic media, including the Internet, regarding the employment history of, and publicly adjudicated disciplinary and enforcement actions against, loan originators.

(8) Establishes a means by which residential mortgage loan originators would, to the greatest extent possible, be required to act in the best interests of the consumer.

(9) Facilitates responsible behavior in the subprime mortgage market place and provides comprehensive training and examination requirements related to subprime mortgage lending.

(10) Facilitates the collection and disbursement of consumer complaints on behalf of State and Federal mortgage regulators.

12 U.S.C. § 5106. System of registration administration by Federal agencies

(a) Development

(1) In general

The Bureau shall develop and maintain a system for registering employees of a depository institution, employees of a subsidiary that is owned and controlled by a depository institution and regulated by a Federal banking agency, or employees of an institution regulated by the Farm Credit Administration, as registered loan originators with the Nationwide Mortgage Licensing System and Registry. The system shall be implemented before the end of the 1-year period beginning on the date of enactment of the Consumer Financial Protection Act of 2010.

(2) Registration requirements

In connection with the registration of any loan originator under this subsection, *the Bureau* shall, at a minimum, furnish or cause to be furnished to the Nationwide Mortgage Licensing System and Registry information concerning the *identity of the employee,* including—

    (A) fingerprints for submission to the Federal Bureau of Investigation, and any governmental agency or entity authorized to receive such information for a State and national criminal history background check; and

    (B) personal history and experience, including authorization for the Nationwide Mortgage Licensing System and Registry to obtain information related to any administrative, civil or criminal findings by any governmental jurisdiction.

(b) Coordination

(1) Unique identifier

The Federal banking agencies, *and the Bureau of Consumer Financial Protection* shall coordinate with the Nationwide Mortgage Licensing System and Registry to establish protocols for assigning a unique identifier to each registered loan originator that will facilitate electronic tracking and uniform identification of, and public access to, the employment history of and publicly adjudicated disciplinary and enforcement actions against loan originators.

(2) Nationwide Mortgage Licensing System and Registry development

To facilitate the transfer of information required by subsection (a)(2), the Nationwide Mortgage Licensing System and Registry shall coordinate with the Federal banking agencies, through the Financial Institutions Examination Council, and the Farm Credit Administration concerning the development and operation, by such System and Registry, of the registration functionality and data requirements for loan originators.

(c) Consideration of factors and procedures

In establishing the registration procedures under subsection (a) and the protocols for assigning a unique identifier to a registered loan originator, the Federal banking agencies shall make such de minimis exceptions as may be appropriate to paragraphs (1)(A) and (2) of section 5103(a) of this title, shall make reasonable efforts to utilize existing information to minimize the burden of registering loan originators, and shall consider methods for automating the process to the greatest extent practicable consistent with the purposes of this title.

Deloitte.

Deloitte & Touche LLP

Suite 800
1750 Tysons Boulevard
McLean, VA 22102-4219
USA

Tel: +1 703 251 1000
Fax: +1 703 251 3400
www.deloitte.com

INDEPENDENT AUDITORS' REPORT

To the Federal Financial Institutions Examination Council:

We have audited the accompanying balance sheets of the Federal Financial Institutions Examination Council (the "Council") as of December 31, 2010 and 2009, and the related statements of revenues and expenses and changes in cumulative results of operations, and cash flows for the years then ended. These financial statements are the responsibility of the Council's management. Our responsibility is to express an opinion on these financial statements based on our audits.

We conducted our audits in accordance with auditing standards generally accepted in the United States of America and the standards applicable to financial audits contained *in Government Auditing Standards* issued by the Comptroller General of the United States. Those standards require that we plan and perform the audit to obtain reasonable assurance about whether the financial statements are free of material misstatement. An audit includes consideration of internal control over financial reporting as a basis for designing audit procedures that are appropriate in the circumstances, but not for the purpose of expressing an opinion on the effectiveness of the Council's internal control over financial reporting. Accordingly, we express no such opinion. An audit also includes examining, on a test basis, evidence supporting the amounts and disclosures in the financial statements, assessing the accounting principles used and significant estimates made by management, as well as evaluating the overall financial statement presentation. We believe that our audits provide a reasonable basis for our opinion.

In our opinion, such financial statements present fairly, in all material respects, the financial position of the Federal Financial Institutions Examination Council as of December 31, 2010 and 2009, and the results of its operations and its cash flows for the years then ended in conformity with accounting principles generally accepted in the United States of America.

In accordance with *Government Auditing Standards*, we have also issued our report dated February 28, 2011, on our consideration of the Council's internal control over financial reporting and our tests of its compliance with certain provisions of laws, regulations, contracts, and grant agreements and other matters. The purpose of that report is to describe the scope of our testing of internal control over financial reporting and compliance and the results of that testing, and not to provide an opinion on the internal control over financial reporting or on compliance. That report is an integral part of an audit performed in accordance with *Government Auditing Standards* and should be considered in assessing the results of our audit.

Deloitte + Touche LLP

February 28, 2011

FEDERAL FINANCIAL INSTITUTIONS EXAMINATION COUNCIL
Balance Sheets

	As of December 31,	
	2010	2009
ASSETS		
CURRENT ASSETS		
Cash	$ 746,815	$ 1,022,700
Accounts receivable from member organizations	1,276,250	1,001,002
Other accounts receivable—net	104,441	90,628
Total current assets	2,127,506	2,114,330
NONCURRENT ASSETS		
Furniture and equipment—at cost	219,484	118,390
Central Data Repository software—at cost	19,371,661	18,231,272
Home Mortgage Disclosure Act Software—at cost	2,783,868	2,344,680
Less accumulated depreciation	(12,704,895)	(10,827,552)
Net capital assets	9,670,118	9,866,790
TOTAL ASSETS	$ 11,797,624	$ 11,981,120
LIABILITIES AND CUMULATIVE RESULTS OF OPERATIONS		
CURRENT LIABILITIES		
Accounts payable and accrued liabilities payable to member organizations	$ 839,152	$ 981,180
Other accounts payable and accrued liabilities	988,059	927,051
Accrued annual leave	27,746	20,117
Capital lease payable	37,828	16,815
Deferred revenue	2,746,667	1,856,180
Total current liabilities	4,639,452	3,801,343
LONG-TERM LIABILITIES		
Capital lease payable	142,202	80,576
Deferred revenue	6,746,128	7,913,219
Deferred rent	6,605	–
Total long-term liabilities	6,894,935	7,993,795
Total liabilities	11,534,387	11,795,138
CUMULATIVE RESULTS OF OPERATIONS	263,237	185,982
TOTAL LIABILITIES AND CUMULATIVE RESULTS OF OPERATIONS	$ 11,797,624	$ 11,981,120

See notes to financial statements.

FEDERAL FINANCIAL INSTITUTIONS EXAMINATION COUNCIL
Statements of Revenues and Expenses and Changes in Cumulative Results of Operations

| | For the years ended December 31, | |
	2010	2009
REVENUES		
Assessments on member organizations	$ 632,344	$ 589,988
Central Data Repository	4,452,286	5,741,157
Home Mortgage Disclosure Act	3,433,075	3,071,973
Tuition	2,662,193	2,322,041
Community Reinvestment Act	1,024,844	1,013,110
Uniform Bank Performance Report	464,633	537,606
Total revenues	12,669,375	13,275,875
EXPENSES		
Data processing	4,529,275	4,370,506
Professional fees	3,635,374	3,674,379
Salaries and related benefits	1,739,031	1,468,414
Depreciation	1,877,343	2,943,660
Rental of office space	264,989	247,648
Administration fees	245,000	245,000
Travel	170,404	156,742
Books and subscriptions	1,656	18,985
Other seminar expenses	30,297	33,343
Rental and maintenance of office equipment	48,313	50,967
Office and other supplies	25,033	14,107
Printing	18,380	19,342
Postage	1,660	1,960
Miscellaneous	5,365	6,011
Total expenses	12,592,120	13,251,064
RESULTS OF OPERATIONS	77,255	24,811
CUMULATIVE RESULTS OF OPERATIONS—Beginning of year	185,982	161,171
CUMULATIVE RESULTS OF OPERATIONS—End of year	$ 263,237	$ 185,982

See notes to financial statements.

FEDERAL FINANCIAL INSTITUTIONS EXAMINATION COUNCIL
Statements of Cash Flows

	For the years ended December 31,	
	2010	2009
CASH FLOWS FROM OPERATING ACTIVITIES		
Results of operations	$ 77,255	$ 24,811
Adjustments to reconcile results of operations to net cash provided by operating activities:		
Depreciation	1,877,343	2,943,660
(Increase) decrease in assets:		
Accounts receivable from member organizations	(275,247)	571,133
Other accounts receivable	(13,812)	14,995
Increase (decrease) in liabilities:		
Accounts payable and accrued liabilities payable to member organizations	(77,379)	(319,538)
Other accounts payable and accrued liabilities	(162,453)	642,017
Accrued annual leave	7,629	(1,891)
Deferred revenue (current and non-current)	(276,603)	(199,161)
Deferred rent	6,605	–
Net cash provided by operating activities	1,163,338	3,676,026
CASH FLOWS FROM INVESTING ACTIVITIES		
Capital expenditures	(1,427,853)	(3,362,003)
CASH FLOWS FROM FINANCING ACTIVITIES		
Capital lease payments	(11,370)	–
NET (DECREASE) INCREASE IN CASH	(275,885)	314,023
CASH BALANCE—Beginning of year	1,022,700	708,677
CASH BALANCE—End of year	$ 746,815	$ 1,022,700

See notes to financial statements.

1. Organization and Purpose

The Federal Financial Institutions Examination Council (the "Council") was established under Title X of the Financial Institutions Regulatory and Interest Rate Control Act of 1978. The purpose of the Council is to prescribe uniform principles and standards for the federal examination of financial institutions and to make recommendations to promote uniformity in the supervision of these financial institutions. The five agencies which were represented on the Council during 2010, referred to hereinafter as member organizations, are as follows:

> Board of Governors of the Federal Reserve System (FRB)
> Federal Deposit Insurance Corporation (FDIC)
> National Credit Union Administration (NCUA)
> Office of the Comptroller of the Currency (OCC)
> Office of Thrift Supervision (OTS)

In accordance with the Financial Services Regulatory Relief Act of 2006, a representative state regulator was added as a full voting member of the Council in October 2006.

The Council was given additional statutory responsibilities by section 340 of the Housing and Community Development Act of 1980, Public Law 96-399. Among these responsibilities are the implementation of a system to facilitate public access to data that depository institutions must disclose under the Home Mortgage Disclosure Act of 1975 (HMDA) and the aggregation of annual HMDA data, by census tract, for each metropolitan statistical area.

On July 21, 2010, the Dodd-Frank Wall Street Reform and Consumer Protection Act of 2010 (Dodd-Frank Act) was signed into law. This legislation substitutes the director of the Consumer Financial Protection Bureau for the director of the Office of Thrift Supervision as a member of the Council effective July 21, 2011.

The Council's financial statements do not include financial data for the Council's Appraisal Subcommittee (the Subcommittee). The Subcommittee was created pursuant to Public Law 101–73, Title XI of the Financial Institutions Reform, Recovery, and Enforcement Act of 1989. Although it is a subcommittee of the Council, the Appraisal Subcommittee maintains separate financial records and administrative processes. The Council is not responsible for any debts incurred by the Subcommittee, nor are Subcommittee funds available for use by the Council.

2. Significant Accounting Policies

The Council prepares its financial statements in accordance with accounting principles generally accepted in the United States of America (GAAP).

Revenues—Assessments are made on member organizations to fund the Council's operations based on expected cash needs. Amounts over- or under- assessed due to differences between actual and expected cash needs are presented in the "Cumulative Results of Operations" line item during the year and then are used to offset or increase the next year's assessment. Deficits in "Cumulative Results of Operations" can be recouped in the following year's assessments.

The Council provides seminars in the Washington, D.C., area and at locations throughout the country for member organizations and other agencies. The Council also coordinates the production and distribution of the Uniform Bank Performance Reports (UBPR) through the FDIC. Tuition and UBPR revenue is adjusted at year-end to match expenses incurred as a result of providing education classes and UBPR services. For differences between revenues and expenses, member agencies are assessed an additional amount or credited a refund based on each member's proportional cost for the Examiner Education and UBPR budget. The Council also recognizes revenue from member agencies for expenses incurred related to the Community Reinvestment Act.

Capital Assets—Furniture and equipment is recorded at cost less accumulated depreciation. Depreciation is calculated on a straight-line basis over the estimated useful lives of the assets, which range from four to ten years. Upon the sale or other disposition of a depreciable asset, the cost and related accumulated depreciation are removed and any gain or loss is recognized. The Central Data Repository (CDR) and the HMDA rewrite, internally developed software projects, are recorded at cost as required by the Internal Use Software Topic of Financial Accounting Standards Board (FASB) Accounting Standards Codification.

Deferred Revenue—Deferred revenue includes cash collected and accounts receivable primarily related to the CDR and HMDA.

Deferred Rent—The lease for office and classroom space contains scheduled rent increases over the term of the lease. As required by the Leases Topic of the FASB Accounting Standards Codification, rent abatements and scheduled rent increases must be considered in determining the annual rent expense to be recognized. The deferred rent represents the difference between the actual lease payments and the rent expense recognized.

Estimates—The preparation of financial statements in conformity with GAAP requires management to make estimates and assumptions that affect the reported amounts of assets and liabilities and the disclosure of contingent assets and liabilities at the date of the financial statements and the reported amounts of revenues and expenses during the reporting period. Actual results could differ from those estimates.

Allowance for Doubtful Accounts—Accounts receivable for non-members are shown net of the allowance for doubtful accounts. Accounts receivable considered uncollectible are charged against the allowance account in the year they are deemed uncollectible. The allowance for doubtful accounts is adjusted monthly, based upon a review of outstanding receivables.

3. Transactions with Member Organizations

	2010	2009
Accounts Receivable		
Board of Governors of the Federal Reserve System	$ 290,047	$ 209,922
Federal Deposit Insurance Corporation	467,726	439,609
National Credit Union Administration	47,501	48,593
Office of the Comptroller of the Currency	416,572	244,883
Office of Thrift Supervision	54,404	57,995
	$ 1,276,250	$ 1,001,002
Accounts Payable and Accrued Liabilities		
Board of Governors of the Federal Reserve System	$ 579,792	$ 618,861
Federal Deposit Insurance Corporation	126,265	247,870
National Credit Union Administration	7,624	20,877
Office of the Comptroller of the Currency	124,321	72,103
Office of Thrift Supervision	1,150	21,469
	$ 839,152	$ 981,180
Operations		
Assessments to member organizations for operating expenses	$ 632,344	$ 589,988
FRB provided administrative support services to the Council at an expense of	245,000	245,000
Member organizations provide data processing services to the Council at an expense of	4,529,275	4,370,506

Notes continue on the following page.

The Council does not directly employ personnel, but rather member organizations detail personnel to support Council operations. These personnel are paid through the payroll systems of member organizations. Salaries and fringe benefits, including retirement benefit plan contributions, are reimbursed to these organizations. The Council does not have any post-retirement or post-employment benefit liabilities since Council personnel are included in the plans of the member organizations.

Member organizations are not reimbursed for the costs of personnel who serve as Council members and on the various task forces and committees of the Council. The value of these contributed services is not included in the accompanying financial statements.

4. Central Data Repository Software

In 2003, the Council entered into an agreement with UNISYS to enhance the methods and systems used to collect, validate, process, and distribute Call Report information, and to store this information in a Central Data Repository (CDR).

The CDR was placed into service in October 2005. At that time, the Council began depreciating the CDR project on the straight-line basis over its estimated useful life of 63 months. In 2009, the Council reevaluated the useful life of CDR and decided to extend the estimated useful life by an additional 36 months based on enhanced functionality of the software. The Council records depreciation expenses and recognizes the same amount of revenue. The value of the CDR asset as of December 31, 2010 and 2009, includes the fully accrued and paid cost.

	2010	2009
Capital Asset CDR		
Beginning balance	$18,231,272	$14,140,655
Software placed in use during the year	1,140,389	4,090,617
Total asset	$19,371,661	$18,231,272

Accounts payable and accrued liabilities related to CDR

Payable to UNISYS for the CDR project	$ 865,630	$ 729,166

Revenues—Central Data Repository—The Council is funding the project by billing the three participating Council member organizations (FRB, FDIC, and OCC). Funding for the years ended December 31, 2010 and 2009, is as follows.

	2010	2009
Deferred Revenue		
Beginning balance	$ 7,424,718	$ 8,173,666
Additions	1,140,389	2,194,713

	2010	2009
Less revenue recognized	(1,856,180)	(2,943,660)
Ending balance	$ 6,708,927	$ 7,424,719
Current portion deferred revenue	$ 2,236,309	$ 1,856,180
Long-term deferred revenue	4,472,618	5,568,539
Total Deferred Revenue	$ 6,708,927	$ 7,424,719

Total CDR Revenue		
Revenue	$ 1,856,180	$ 2,943,660
Hosting and maintenance revenue	2,596,106	2,797,497
Total CDR Revenue	$ 4,452,286	$ 5,741,157

Professionsl Fees		
Hosting and maintenance fees for the CDR project	$ 2,596,106	$ 2,797,497

Depreciation		
Depreciation for the CDR project	$ 1,856,180	$ 2,943,660
Average monthly depreciation	$ 154,682	$ 245,305

5. Home Mortgage Disclosure Act Software

The Council entered into an agreement with FRB to maintain and support the HMDA processing system. In 2007, the Council began a rewrite of the entire HMDA processing system. The HMDA rewrite will enhance the processing system. The cost of the software in process is $2,783,868 and $2,344,680 as of December 31, 2010 and 2009, respectively. The financial activity associated with the processing system for the years ended December 31, 2010 and 2009, is as follows.

	2010	2009
Deferred Revenue		
Beginning balance	$ 2,344,680	1,544,895
Additions	439,188	799,785
Less revenue recognized	0	0
Ending balance	$ 2,783,868	$ 2,344,680
Current portion deferred revenue	$ 556,774	$ 0
Long-term deferred revenue	2,227,094	2,344,680
Total Deferred Revenue	$ 2,783,868	$ 2,344,680

Revenue

The Council recognized the following revenue from member organizations for the production and distribution of reports under the HMDA $ 2,537,870 $ 2,234,514

The Council recognized the following revenue from the Department of Housing and Urban Development's participation in the HMDA project 588,421 559,151

The Council recognized the following revenue from the Mortgage Insurance Companies of America for performing HMDA-related work 306,784 278,308

Total HMDA $ 3,433,075 $ 3,071,973

Depreciation

Depreciation for the HMDA Rewrite project	$ 0	$ 0
Average monthly depreciation	$ 0	$ 0

6. Operating Leases

The FRB, on behalf of the Council, entered into two operating leases at market value to secure office and classroom space. One lease terminated in 2009 and one began in January 2010 with the FDIC.

Years ending December 31	Amount
2011	$ 261,598
2012	264,900
2013	268,292
2014	271,772
Total minimum lease payments	$ 1,066,562

Rental expenses under these operating leases were $264,989 and $247,648 as of December 31, 2010 and 2009, respectively.

7. Capital Leases

In December 2009 and November 2010, the Council entered into capital leases for printing equipment. Furniture and equipment includes $198,485 for the capital leases. Contingent rentals for excess usage of the printing equipment amounted to $11,049 in 2010.

The future minimum lease payments required under the capital leases and the present value of the net minimum lease payments as of December 31, 2010, are as follows:

Years ending December 31	Amount
2011	$ 59,089
2012	59,089
2013	59,089
2014	59,089
2015	31,737

Total minimum lease payments	268,093
Less amount representing maintenance	(72,789)
Net minimum lease payments	195,304
Less amount representing interest	(15,274)
Net minimum lease payments	180,030
Less current maturities of capital lease payments	(37,828)
Long-term capital lease obligations	$ 142,202

8. Subsequent Events

There were no subsequent events that require adjustments to or disclosures in the financial statements as of December 31, 2010. Subsequent events were evaluated through February 28, 2011, which is the date the financial statements were available to be issued.

Deloitte.

Deloitte & Touche LLP

Suite 800
1750 Tysons Boulevard
McLean, VA 22102-4219
USA

Tel: +1 703 251 1000
Fax: +1 703 251 3400
www.deloitte.com

INDEPENDENT AUDITORS' REPORT ON INTERNAL CONTROL OVER FINANCIAL REPORTING AND ON COMPLIANCE AND OTHER MATTERS BASED ON AN AUDIT OF FINANCIAL STATEMENTS PERFORMED IN ACCORDANCE WITH GOVERNMENT AUDITING STANDARDS

To the Federal Financial Institutions Examination Council:

We have audited the financial statements of the Federal Financial Institutions Examination Council (the "Council") as of and for the year ended December 31, 2010, and have issued our report thereon dated February 28, 2011. We conducted our audit in accordance with auditing standards generally accepted in the United States of America and the standards applicable to financial audits contained in *Government Auditing Standards*, issued by the Comptroller General of the United States.

Internal Control over Financial Reporting

In planning and performing our audit, we considered the Council's internal control over financial reporting as a basis for designing our auditing procedures for the purpose of expressing our opinion on the financial statements, but not for the purpose of expressing an opinion on the effectiveness of the Council's internal control over financial reporting. Accordingly, we do not express an opinion on the effectiveness of the Council's internal control over financial reporting.

A *control deficiency* exists when the design or operation of a control does not allow management or employees, in the normal course of performing their assigned functions, to prevent or detect misstatements on a timely basis. A significant deficiency is a control deficiency, or combination of control deficiencies, that adversely affects the entity's ability to initiate, authorize, record, process, or report financial data reliably in accordance with generally accepted accounting principles such that there is more than a remote likelihood that a misstatement of the Council's financial statements that is more than inconsequential will not be prevented or detected by the Council's internal control.

A *material weakness* is a significant deficiency, or combination of significant deficiencies, that results in more than a remote likelihood that a material misstatement of the financial statements will not be prevented or detected by the Council's internal control.

Our consideration of internal control over financial reporting was for the limited purpose described in the first paragraph of this section and would not necessarily identify all deficiencies in internal control that might be significant deficiencies or material weaknesses. We did not identify any deficiencies in internal control over financial reporting that we consider to be material weaknesses, as defined above.

Compliance and Other Matters

As part of obtaining reasonable assurance about whether the Council's financial statements are free of material misstatement, we performed tests of its compliance with certain provisions of laws, regulations, contracts, and grant agreements, noncompliance with which could have a direct and material effect on the determination of financial statement amounts. However, providing an opinion on compliance with those provisions was not an objective of our audit, and accordingly, we do not express such an opinion. The results of our tests disclosed no instances of noncompliance or other matters that are required to be reported under *Government Auditing Standards*.

Distribution

This report is intended solely for the information and use of the Council, management, and others within the organization, and the Office of Inspector General, and the United States Congress, and is not intended to be and should not be used by anyone other than these specified parties.

Deloitte + Touche LLP

February 28, 2011

APPENDIX C: MAPS OF AGENCY REGIONS AND DISTRICTS

THE FEDERAL RESERVE SYSTEM DISTRICTS

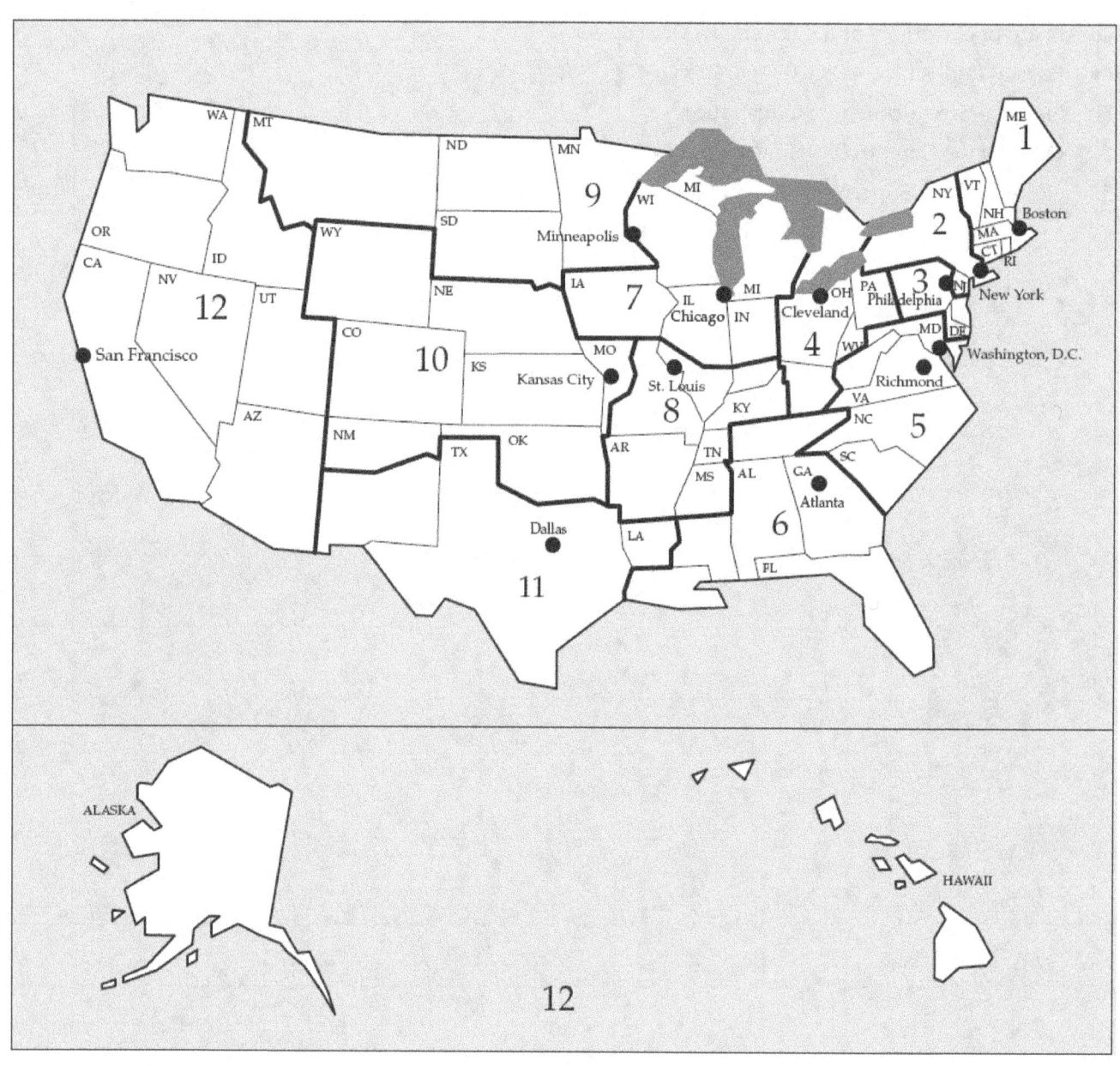

FEDERAL DEPOSIT INSURANCE CORPORATION REGIONS (SUPERVISION AND COMPLIANCE)

* Two area offices are located in Boston
(reports to New York) and Memphis
(reports to Dallas)

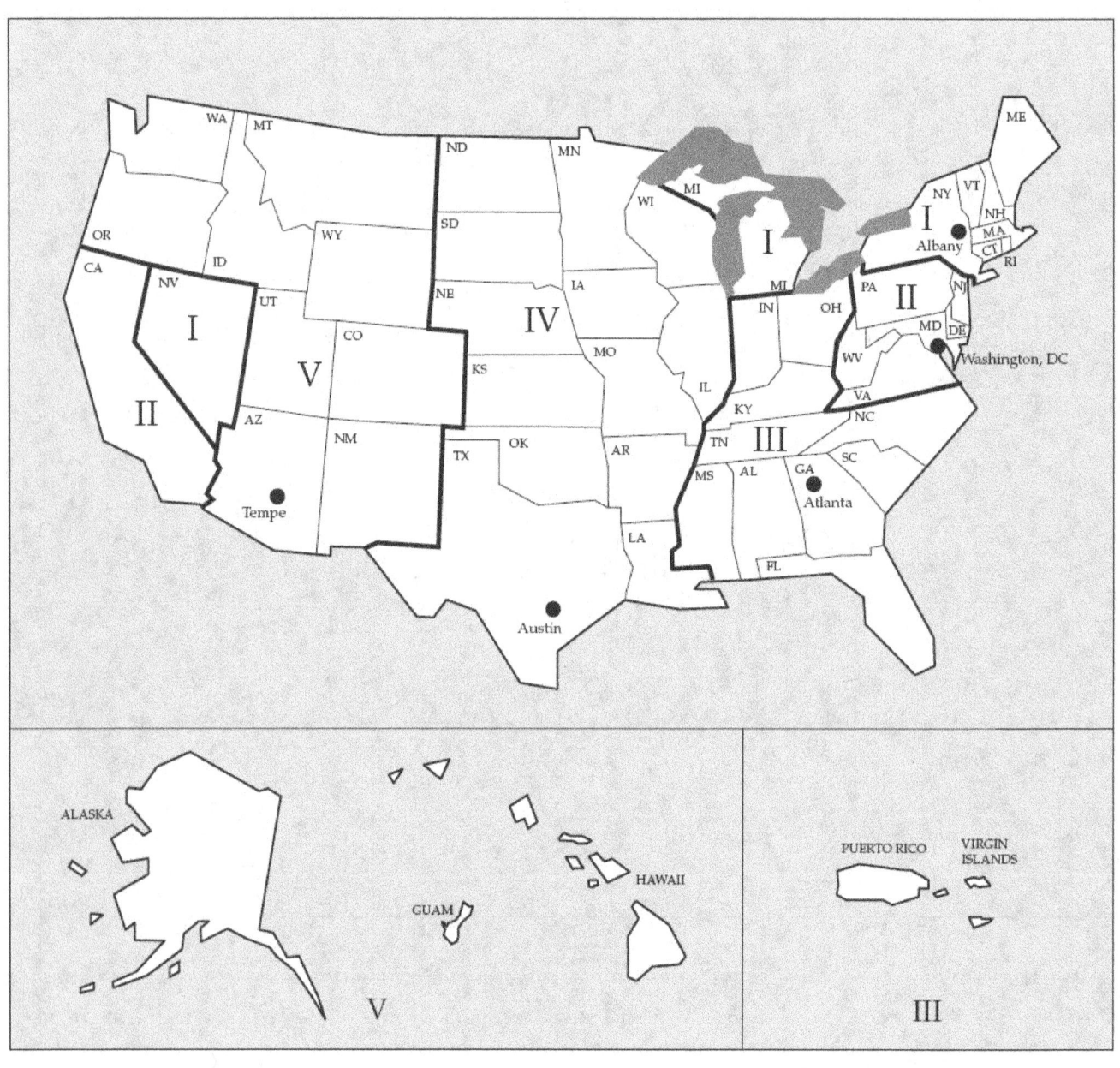

COMPTROLLER OF THE CURRENCY
DISTRICT ORGANIZATION

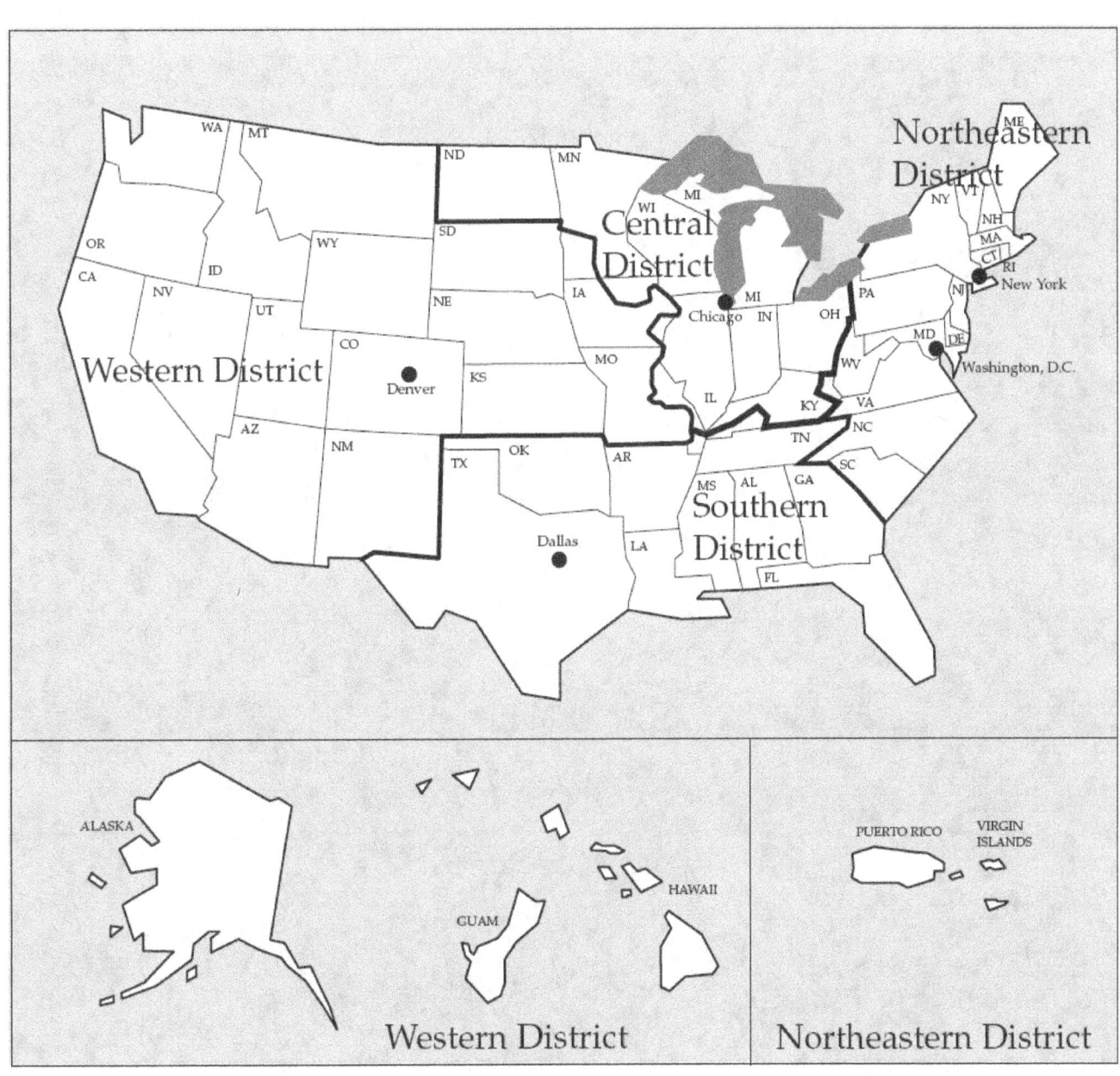

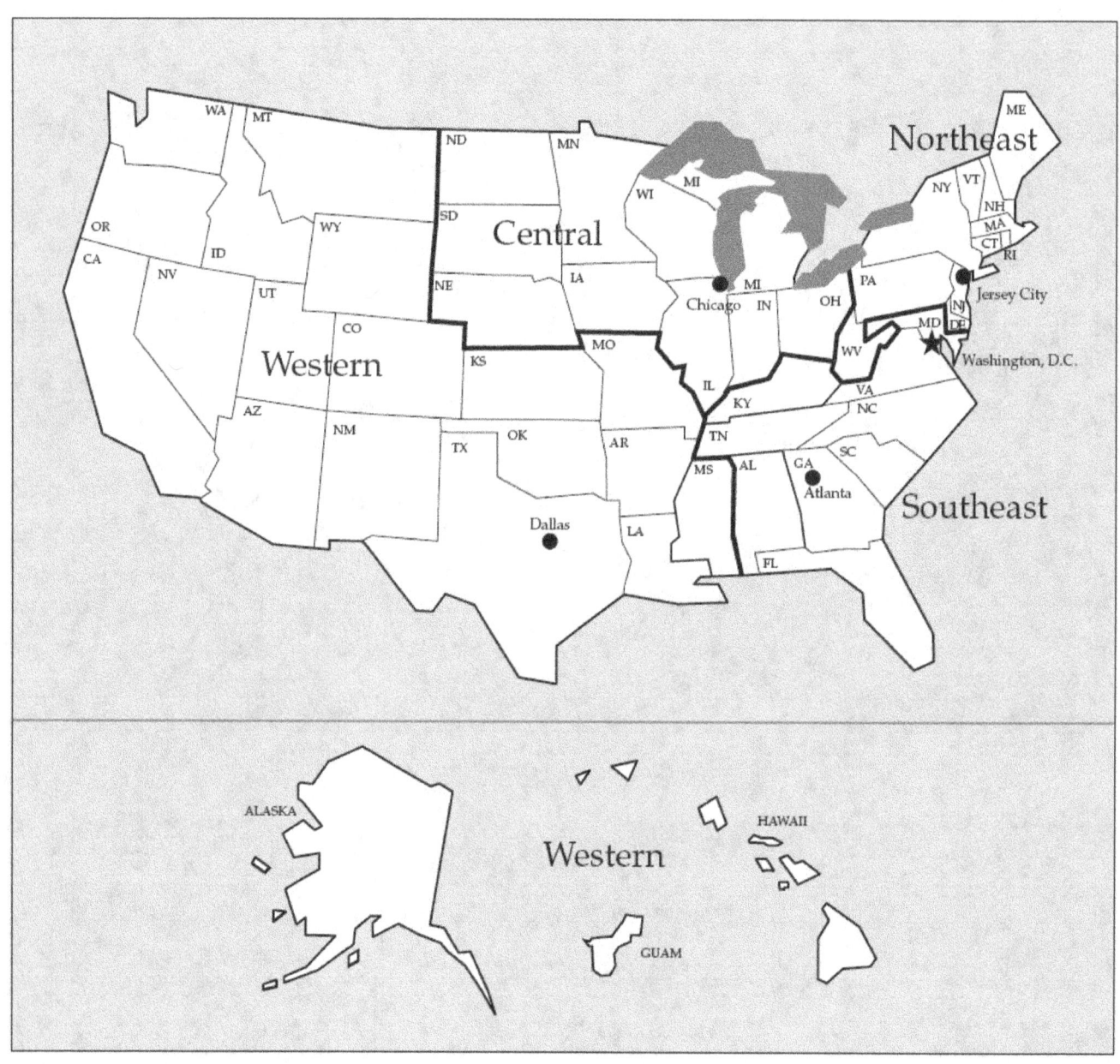

APPENDIX D: ORGANIZATIONAL LISTING OF PERSONNEL

Organization, December 31, 2010

Members of the Council

Sheila C. Bair, *Chairman*
Chairperson
Federal Deposit Insurance
Corporation (FDIC)

John E. Bowman, *Vice Chairman*
Acting Director
Office of Thrift Supervision
(OTS)

Debbie Matz
Chairman
National Credit Union
Administration (NCUA)

John Walsh
Acting Comptroller of the
Currency
Office of the Comptroller of the
Currency (OCC)

Daniel K. Tarullo
Member
Board of Governors of the
Federal Reserve System (FRB)

John Munn
State Liaison Committee (SLC)
Chairman
Director
Nebraska Department of
Banking & Finance

State Liaison Committee (SLC)

John Munn, *Chairman*
Director
Nebraska Department of
Banking & Finance

David Cotney
Commissioner
Massachusetts Division of Banks

Harold E. Feeney
Commissioner
Texas Credit Union Department

Douglas Foster
Commissioner
Texas Department of Savings
and Mortgage Lending

Charles A. Vice
Commissioner
Kentucky Department of
Financial Institutions

Council Staff Officer

Paul T. Sanford
Executive Secretary

Interagency Staff Groups

Agency Liaison Group

Sandra Thompson (FDIC)
Thomas A. Barnes (OTS)
Melinda Love (NCUA)
Timothy Long (OCC)
Arthur W. Lindo (FRB)
Michael Stevens (SLC Chair
Representative)

Legal Advisory Group

Michael H. Krimminger, *Chairman*
(FDIC)
Deborah Dakin (OTS)
Robert M. Fenner (NCUA)
Julie L. Williams (OCC)
Scott Alvarez, (FRB)
Christopher Young (SLC Chair
Representative)

Task Force on Consumer Compliance

David Cotney, *Chairman* (SLC
Chair Representative)
Luke H. Brown (FDIC)
Moisette Green (NCUA)
Calvin Hagins (OCC)
Joel Palmer (OTS)
Paul Robin (FRB)

Task Force on Examiner Education

Dana E. Payne, *Chairman* (FRB)
Timothy Segerson, *Vice Chairman*
(NCUA)
Charlotte Buchanan (SLC Chair
Representative)
Cheryl Davis (OCC)
Dave Freimuth (OTS)
Philip D. Mento (FDIC)

Task Force on Information Sharing

Michael Kraemer, *Chairman* (FRB)
Dave Godwin (OTS)
John Kolhoff (SLC Chair
Representative)
Charles Lacek (FDIC)
Robin Stefan (OCC)
Catherine Yao (NCUA)

Task Force on Reports

Robert F. Storch, *Chairman* (FDIC)
James Caton (OTS)
Kyle Thomas (Acting SLC Chair
Representative)
Arthur W. Lindo (FRB)
Kathy K. Murphy (OCC)
Virginia L. Phillips (NCUA)

Task Force on Supervision

Thomas A. Barnes, *Chairman* (OTS)
Timothy Long (OCC)
Patrick M. Parkinson (FRB)
Timothy Segerson (NCUA)
Sandra Thompson (FDIC)
Charles A. Vice (SLC Chair
Representative)

Task Force on Surveillance Systems

Robin Stefan, *Chairman* (OCC)
Bob Bacon (SLC Chair
Representative)
James Caton (OTS)
Charles Collier (FDIC)
Matt Mattson (FRB)
Virginia L. Phillips (NCUA)

Staff Members of the FFIEC

Shown are the FFIEC staff members at the Seidman Center in Arlington, Virginia, where they have their offices and classrooms for examiner education programs.

Federal Financial Institutions Examination Council staff members (from the left to right): Rosanna Piccirilli, Ernie Larkins, Cathy Pritchard, David Vallee, John Smullen, Darlene Callis, Michelle Clark, Karen Smith, Juliet Pradier, Cynthia Curry-Daniel, Paul Sanford, Melanie Middleton, and Jennifer Herring.